Other Reader's Say:

"Rick Prigmore's **The Joy of Living** is an exhilarating romp for the spirit!!! Join a celebration of life from a man 'with a license of a higher order of being'. Rick's sole mission is to experience and share life joyfully, which he does passionately and with great perception.

Rick's 'feel good' stories may not cure your problems, but they're better than chicken soup - they're a box of chocolates for the spirit!!"

Anita Bergen, author of "Life and Other Options", Atlanta, Georgia

"Rick Prigmore's stories are full of life affirming qualities. They are reflective of the work he has done through the Universal Brotherhood Movement and the positive contributions he has made to the world."

Dan Liss, Editor, "Aquarius", (a New Age newspaper), Atlanta, Georgia

"Rick Prigmore is the greatest, happiest guy I've ever known. When you ask him how he is doing, he always says, "Better and Better, every day in every way" - and he really means it. If you really want to feel exhilarated, read this book - it's the next best thing to the joy of knowing Rick."

Marty Zevin, author of "How To Settle Your Own Personal Injury Case"; Chairman of the Florida Chapter of Holistic Lawyers, Florida

"Fasten your seat belts for the most joyful ride of your life. This is what life is all about - JOY! "The Joy of Living" is just that! This book is a romp through life with a man who knows how to live productively, successfully and with a great heart."
Dr. Delia Sellers, Publisher, "Abundant Living" magazine, Prescott, Arizona

"In his book, "The Joy of Living", Rick Prigmore, a friend and role model for some 22 years, puts into print the wonderful things God does, but sometimes we miss. Must Reading!"
Orazio "o.mike" Fichera, Publisher, Margate, Florida

"Be prepared for your heart to be fully opened with a gloriously light touch. Belly laughs and life lessons go hand in hand in Rick Prigmore's "The Joy of Living". I loved it!"
Robert A. Barnes, author, "The Blue Dolphin", England

"You will enjoy and benefit by reading Rick's stories. He is a proven successful leader, teacher and role model. For more than half a century, while conducting business on six continents, I would often pause in negotiations and ask myself, 'How would Rick handle this opportunity successfully in a foreign culture?' You will profit in many ways by reading "The Joy of Living". "
Willis R. Wolf, Chairman and CEO, Flow Corp., Akron, Ohio

"I am enriched when I read the life experience stories that Rick Prigmore chooses to share with others. I never fail to be amazed by the gems of wisdom, as well as the tales of fun, intrigue, inspiration, passion and sometimes tragedy, that are part of every human being's experience. Congratulations on getting your stories ready to share with others."
Rev. Brian McCutcheon, Publisher, "Synchronicity Magazine", Calgary, Alberta, Canada

To Rick, Follow your dream,
Live every day of your
life to the fullest!!!
Be joyful...
Rick Prigmore
9/3/03

The Joy of Living

by

Richard D. "Rick" Prigmore

The Joy of Living

by Richard D. Prigmore

Published by:

Bright Angel Press
Atlanta, Georgia

Cover Design by:

Darleen Claire Wodzenski
Advance Wellness Center of Buckhead
Atlanta, Georgia

ISBN 0-9661708-0-6

Contents

The Early Years; circa 1930's and 1940's

The Middle Years; circa 1950's and 1960's

The Mature Years; circa 1970's

The Vagabond Years; circa 1980's

More Vagabond Years; circa 1980's

Home Again; circa 1980's and 1990's

Postscript

Dedicated To

my inspiration, my teacher, my critic, my stabilizer, my lifemate,
the supporter of my dreams,

+ −

+ - is a symbol representing the French expression,
" Qu' Hier, Que Demain "

Translated into English it means...

"I love you more than yesterday, but less than tomorrow"

Audio Book by the Author

" The Joy of Living - *in Stereo* "

Recorded by Richard D. Prigmore

Sound Engineer, Arthur Holbrook
Stampede Studios
Atlanta, Georgia

Cover Design - Darleen Claire Wodzenski
Advance Wellness Center of Buckhead
Atlanta, Georgia

Acknowledgments

This book may not have been written were it not for the urging and encouragement of my friend, Dr. John Harricharan. John has written several bestsellers. His advice was, "If I can do it, you can do it too."

"But, John," I questioned, "what do I have to write about?"

"With your life it should be easy", he responded. "Just write stories of your experiences as you remember them. Your stories are shining examples of the dignity of the human spirit."

Once started, my beloved life mate, Jeni, enthusiastically endorsed my efforts and gave me confidence. Each story seemed easier to record.

My profound thanks to John, the initiator, to Jeni, the nurturer (She added the fertilizer to the soil of inertia.) and to the ever-so-perceptive Anita Bergen for her diligent monitoring and correction of my spelling and syntax. The hours she has spent typing, editing, formatting, correcting, counseling and advising me have been invaluable to the production of this book.

Additional thanks go to Marty Zevin, Martine Muffon, Barbara Roberts, Colin Tipping, Darleen Claire Wodzenski, Linda Berman, for their invaluable assistance in reading, correcting and advising me as a new venturer into the arena of published works. My thanks also go to all those, named and unnamed, who participated in this tapestry of life, recorded as I have remembered. Who I am today is, in a major way, the culmination of associations with these VIP's in my life. Thanks to all of you!

Introduction

by John Harricharan

I first met Rick Prigmore many years ago. He was standing outside an auditorium where I had just finished giving a lecture. Even then, as someone introduced us, I recognized the spiritual stature of this outgoing, uplifting man. Oh, you know the type, you can't leave their presence without a smile on your face. Over the years, through ups and downs, we kept in touch and now here is Rick, writing a really wonderful book about the joy of living. On this topic, Rick is a professional. He continually manages to bring joy to *every* situation.

Rick is a shining example of the message and the messenger being one. He exudes such love, compassion and understanding that no matter what your dilemma, you are moved to go on and overcome the obstacles blocking your progress. Here, in these stories, Rick offers us a part of himself and his life that have rarely been shared before. Some of Rick's literary sketches will leave you with a laugh and still others with a tear trickling down your cheek. But, in every case, you will find yourself not wanting the book to end.

"The Joy of Living" is a collection of stories about life and living . You'll want to to keep it in your library or on your coffee table, because you'll be referring to these tales time and again, whenever you need a lift. Perhaps, in reading these stories, you will discover a secret that Rick Prigmore has been practicing for years - that life has no meaning, but that it is *you* who bring true meaning to life. Thank you, Rick, for sharing "The Joy of Living" with us.

John Harricharan

FOREWORD

I am having a wonderful life! My physical health is excellent; my marriage of more than a quarter century to my life mate, Jeni, is all I could ask for or imagine; my economic health is stable and adequate. No one could have a finer family support system, embraced by more than fifty family members, two-thirds of them "heart adopted". There are probably others who are just as fortunate. I sincerely hope so.

At the urging of many friends, I have set down some stories from my life. I have done so, not so much for others to read, but to enhance my own memory of the events that have shaped my life.

I hasten to point out that these chronicles and vignettes make no claim to being historically accurate. They are told as I remember them, admittedly recalled through the prism of my eternal optimism.

If I had not-so-happy experiences, and I must have; *if* I failed to meet society's expectations at times, and I probably did; *if* there are those in my history who hold less than pleasant thoughts of me, and there probably are; the "feather-pillow" envelope of time has muffled the memory.

I choose to view the sunrise of life each day in the vibrant rainbow spectrum of joy, thanksgiving, wonder, appreciation and expectation. It is ever a new dawn. So, I pen these glimpses, not as a philosopher, teacher, moralist or educator, but as a chronicler of some mostly happy times. Enjoy.

What's Your Ornery Quotient?

Did you ever do anything ornery when you were a kid? I mean something you knew was wrong but did it anyway to impress your brother — or girl friend — or someone? Well, I have - more than once.

My brother, John, and I made wooden pistols with spring clothespin triggers that shot rubber bands, big rubber bands cut from inner tubes. (In the old days all the tires had rubber inner tubes). They made great 'bullets'. We played a lot of cowboys and Indians at that time. (Now I just read about cowboys and Indians in western novels.)

One summer evening we were down the road toward Leon a quarter mile or so from the house. We lived in Pickrell Corners then, 25 miles east of Wichita. It was dark with little moonlight and we must have been sneaking up on a bunch of Apaches. The weeds along the narrow, two lane road grew right up to the driving space and hadn't been mowed in weeks. It made great cover.

We heard a car coming while we were crouched out of sight. I whispered to John, "Buffalo."

He nodded wisely (I think). We checked our guns and made ready to shoot the great beast. As it roared by we aimed for the 'heart spot' behind the foreleg, (it really was the fender) and pulled the triggers. The 'beast' swerved, hit the brakes and skidded to a stop. In an instant were long gone on a dead run for home. We set a record for getting undressed and into bed, quietly.

Next day a neighbor stopped in and asked Dad if his boys

had 'lost' any rubber bands. Luckily he was a friendly neighbor, because one of our 'shots' had sailed into the open window and popped him on the side of the head. (Must have been John's because I shot for the heart.)

When we got our impounded weapons back - a long time later - we hunted buffalo farther from the road. A much worse 'ornery' occurred later when we should have known better. John did, and tried to talk me out of it. Here's what happened:

It was winter and we were running our trapline a half mile north of Pickrell Corner near the railroad. We had not caught hide nor hare. John, who was always a better shot than I, was carrying the 20 gauge. Up jumped a jack rabbit and opened his throttle to the max, running belly-to-the-ground. John lined up on him, swung the gun smoothly past him and pulled the trigger. The load caught him mid stride. He folded, flopped and skidded thirty feet. That John boy could shoot!

Mom wouldn't cook jack rabbit. Too tough, she said. So we carried it along for no good reason as we walked the railroad tracks toward the highway underpass. I spotted a pickup coming like a bat out of Hades and said to my brother, "Bet I can drop him into the pickup bed as he goes under the railroad."

"Don't do it," John advised.

But, I was supremely confident and very stupid. I gauged the speed, the distance, the height of the trestle above the highway and, as the pickup zoomed out of sight, I dropped the rabbit.

Out came the vehicle - down plunged the rabbit - I had miscalculated. It hit the windshield right in front of the driver. He swerved and skidded back and forth trying to stay upright. Needless to say, we left the scene in Olympic time.

I still remember some new words I learned that day as the livid driver screamed and cussed us. We kept out of sight a long time after that episode just in case he came looking for us.

Wow! That was really a dumb thing to do.

Clyde's Bounty

We needed a new tire for the Model 'A' Ford and had no money to buy one. The dollar a week we got for hauling a kid we'll call 'Clyde' to high school with us was just enough for gas. Our trap line hadn't produced any skunk hides to sell and we were worried about the blister that developed on the right rear tire. What to do?

Monday morning we headed for school in El Dorado, ten miles away, with no small amount of trepidation. A mile and a half up the road we picked up Clyde. He was all smiles. He pulled out his wallet to give us his dollar for the week and John spotted a couple of tens in it. $$$$

Now, that family was no better off financially than the Prigmore's, so those tens looked like the Denver mint.

"Where'd ya get all that money?" John asked, with little diplomacy.

"I sold my pig that I've been feeding. Brought $21," he grinned.

John looked at me and I looked at John. Both of us saw dollar signs and a new tire.

"Look, Clyde," I intoned smoothly, "There's twenty more weeks of school left this year. Why don't you just go ahead and pay the full 20 weeks and that way you don't have to worry about having a ride until school's out."

Clyde wasn't destined for an Oxford scholarship. That's why, behind his back, his peers called him, 'house ape'. He looked skeptical.

It took a lot of salesmanship to get him to part with that twenty so we could buy the tire. But he did — and we did — and we *all* had transportation until school was out. As I recall, we had to 'borrow' a little 'drip gas' from the oil field compressor down the road - but that's another story.

Rickerisms - Bits of Whizdom

It Wasn't My Time

I never was one to tell war stories about 'The Big One' back in the mid-40's. But, a few times our kids got me started reminiscing about my small part and it always seemed downright remarkable I made it through. Take the case of Porter (not his real name):

We had waded ashore from landing craft on Leyte beach in the Philippines following General McArthur's 'we shall return' promise made three years earlier. More than 600 ships of all descriptions lay at anchor in the bay lighting the night skies with tracers searching for Japanese bombers radar insisted were there. We crouched in quickly dug foxholes, more afraid of the friendly fire than the strafing Zeros 50 feet overhead.

Our hastily built airstrip, purchased with lives of many marines, infantry, engineers and Seabees, attracted 'bogies' like flies to honey. For nine days we fueled and armed fighter planes, based far to the rear, flying sorties against the enemy from our Tacloban strip. About every 20 minutes, day and night, we were strafed or bombed. Our camp, just off the end of the strip on the same narrow peninsula, was extremely vulnerable.

One early morning, following a quickly swallowed breakfast of powdered eggs and coffee, we headed for the strip to preflight the P-51's for dawn patrol. Porter loved to drive the open-air jeep and would often skip breakfast to wait in the driver's seat for the rest of us to eat. Except for this morning.

As we ran up to the jeep, Porter slid over to the right seat with the comment, "Rick, why don't you drive this morning?"

All the guys were astounded and ripped him with comical comments because this behavior was so atypical. We piled in and I had just turned onto the road which lined up with the strip a few hundred yards ahead when someone yelled,

"Hit the dirt!!"

Here came a Zero, guns blazing, headed at us 50 feet above the coconut palms. I hit the brakes, killed the engine and fell out of the driver's side into a ditch. Porter, riding where I usually rode, bailed out on the right. He caught a 20 mm cannon shell with my name on it. Why he chose that morning to let me drive no one will ever know.

So, here I am, a half century later, still enjoying life because of a twist of fate. It just wasn't my time.

Wrong Way Crane

A few days after we had waded ashore at Tacloban on our return to the Philippines, we were on the temporary airstrip servicing P-38's and P-51's to fly support missions over our marines and infantry across the island. Near constant air attacks kept us hopping from cockpit to bomb craters a few steps away. Harry Weekly, my buddy, and I stationed 'Crane', a raw boned, natural Oklahoman from deep in the scrub oak country, to watch for enemy planes while we preflighted the P-38's. One night Crane told us, as we were sitting around the campfire where I was making cocoa, "Ya know, I once drove sixty miles into Oklahoma City to a violin concert. All it was was some guy playin' the fiddle." That was Crane.

Suddenly, all hell broke loose as the air buzzed with lead from a strafing Zero and from ships in the bay shooting at it. We bailed out of our cockpits and dove for the nearest crater, flattening against the sand. A large object landed behind us in the bottom of the crater. We waited with breath poised for the 'bomb' to explode and blow us to kingdom come. Nothing happened. Then, out of the pit came sputtered curses as Crane, who had projectiled from his watch station into the crater, muttered, "The S.O.B. came in from the wrong direction."

Earlier passes had come in from the north and that's where Crane was watching. He never thought to look both directions. It's amazing how quickly the tension breaks and we laughed at his actions. From that day forward he was labeled, 'Wrong Way Crane.'

Econ 101

C.I.F. - That's the first economic principle I learned in College. It was powerful - and I remember it to this day.

I had returned from WW II, reentered the work force at Beech Aircraft and was prepared to build Bonanzas, Model 18's and Staggerwings until retirement. Mom wanted me to go to college under the G.I. bill. Dad and my "Santa Fe railroad" uncles, who had been "successful" without education beyond high school, advised me to grab the "bird in the hand" and forget the "bird in the bush."

I opted for the closer bird and accepted Beech's "returning-veterans-former-employee" offer. I was hooked into a lifetime of "economic security" - I thought.

The best laid plans........ 2 1/2 months later Beech cut production, restructured their future and laid off a bunch of workers - including me. Re-evaluation time.

I looked at the possibilities and decided no one could fire me if I was 'boss'. Therefore, I needed education to get into that position. So I enrolled in the Summer term of the University of Wichita School of Business to learn to be a boss. That's how I happened to be sitting in the front row of ECO 101 as Dr. Robert Ryan stood at "parade rest," hands clasped behind his back, surveying his freshman class of neophytes.

"Students," he intoned, "You will assimilate much information in your pursuit of a degree in business administration. None will be of greater use to you as you go through life than the principle I'm about to give you now. You can learn manage-

8

ment strategies, personnel handling, accounting techniques, marketing and advertising ploys, products, processes, service rendering and budgeting. NONE will contribute to your success more than the principle of C.I.F. Listen and remember.

"C.I.F. means ------ C A S H I N F I S T!!!! The lubrication of the economy, the measure of success, the essential ingredient of the economic process is M O N E Y ! You can invent the finest product; you can design the most efficient system; you can evaluate the most productive markets; but, if you don't make sales and get the C.I.F., nothing else matters. In business, the rewards go to the 'producers' of C.I.F. Success is measured by 'capital Ss' with vertical lines through them - dollar signs. Although dollars are not *wealth*, they are the *measure* of wealth, the barometer of business, the heart beat of the stock market. C.I.F. is your watchword. Remember it!"

I have never forgotten.

Forty Below

I had never even heard of hunting mountain lions in Utah until Bob Clark called to say his W.T.B. (war time buddy), Ed Connolly, had invited him to go on such a hunt. We had Christmas vacation coming up from Wichita University and decided to go. It was an unforgettable experience.

Just getting from Wichita to Salt Lake City was an adventure in the dead of winter. We drove through Denver in sinister snow, dared to plunge on through Idaho Springs and Clear Creek Canyon, then crept up Berthoud Pass. By the time we had nursed the Buick over the top at more than 11,000 feet altitude we figured we were past the worst of it.

No one had warned us about Rabbit Ears Pass. It was not as high as Berthoud but far more vicious in a blizzard. Just when we decided it was impassable, a snow plow came along and we followed it. The chains we had bought in Denver lasted until we got almost into Utah before a link broke and they were scrap.

After more than 1,100 miles of non-stop driving we reached Ed's house. He was packed and ready. The four of us, including Ed's brother, Wally, piled into a vintage panel truck with all our gear, food and, most important, a quart of Kentucky's best bourbon wrapped protectively in a bath towel. Last to go in on top of everything were the three lion hounds.

Mac was a Walker dog, dumb but vocal; Lucifer was a blue tick, short on nose but a savage asset at the tree; Chico was a black and tan bitch with more trail savvy than all of us.

Our destination was a telephone line cabin high up near

the top of Lost Creek Canyon. It was locked for the winter, when all intelligent folks stayed out of the mountains. But, Ed had talked someone out of a key. We chugged up Parley's Canyon, turned off at Echo Junction and drove on through Hennifer, stopping at the general store for last minute candy bars and sodas.

"Where 'ya headed?" the proprietor asked.

"Up Lost Creek to chase mountain lions," Ed responded enthusiastically.

"Don't get snowed in," was the cautious advice. "It's getting colder and another storm is on the way."

"We'll watch it," Ed said absently. We were too charged up to worry about a little weather. When has youth ever been cautious?

It was late afternoon as we "chained up" and climbed the steep road for seventeen miles to the line cabin. It was a sixteen-foot square beauty, well built and equipped. There were four bunks against the four outside walls with a table and chairs surrounding a pot-bellied stove in the middle of the room. A thermometer outside the door read zero and dropping. We unloaded our gear only to find a major disaster. The hounds, in their scrambling around the back of the truck during the trip, had dislodged the stopper from the booze bottle. All the good stuff had drained out into the towel. Nary a drop left.

That incident didn't bother Wally or me - we didn't imbibe. But, both Ed and Bob were devastated. They decided to go back down to Hennifer next morning to replenish the "necessity." Meanwhile, they took turns chewing on the bourbon-soaked towel.

As we commented on how cold it was getting, Wally began to worry that he might have a "nature's call" in the middle of the night and need to venture out. The more he stewed about it the more worried he became. The rest of us didn't help the situation, commenting on what might or might not get frost-bitten. Sure enough, about bedtime, the urge overtook him and he had to go. He folded some "T-paper," which he held in his teeth, edged over to the door, dropped his pants and lunged outside. I swear, he was back in thirty seconds chattering and shaking as he pulled up his pants. We shook with laughter.

Our planning wasn't the best because our food staple was chili with beans heated on the stove. Ed had been feeding the hounds raw meat, which caused them to expel a lot of gas, too. So, four chili-beaned guys and three flatulent dogs made that sixteen foot square cabin almost untenable. We opted to stay in and suffer rather than escape outside and freeze.

You want to know how cold it got that night? When we climbed into out sleeping bags about 10 p.m. the coffee pot was boiling on the stove. The stove pipe was cherry red halfway to the roof. At three a.m. my chattering teeth awakened me. I had brought only a summer weight sleeping bag. I climbed out to rekindle the fire and discovered the coffee was frozen in the pot! It was that frigid.

I stayed up and fed the fire so we could keep warm. Dawn finally arrived. The windows were iced over an inch thick. Frost crystals hung in the air (frozen humidity). Occasionally a tree would split with a crash as the sap froze and expanded.

Bundled in everything we brought to wear, we made a perfunctory search for lion tracks before deciding to head down to Hennifer to replace the bottle. Ed climbed into the truck and turned the switch. There was a halfhearted groan and no more. The crankcase oil was too stiff to move. We tried to drain the radiator and heat the antifreeze. The drain cock was jammed. What to do? Were we stranded for the winter?

Dauntless youth prevailed. The truck belonged to the University of Utah (it was a part of Ed's Master's program - research) so we figured it could be expendable, if necessary, to "rescue" us.

"Let's build a fire and roll the truck over it so the engine oil will heat up," Ed suggested.

"Sounds like a hot idea," I responded.

So Wally brought some already burning sticks from the stove and we added sage brush. Then, using some lodge pole pine logs and no small degree of ingenuity, we levered the truck forward until the fire was burning under the oil pan. In a few minutes Ed turned the switch and it reluctantly groaned into life. We knew the radiator was frozen so we totally covered the front with cardboard and set out on that seventeen mile trip down the hill.

In less than a mile the radiator was spouting like Old Faithful and the temp gauge was in the red. So, for the next sixteen miles we alternately coasted and chugged until we pulled into the only auto repair shop in that little town. The thermometer on the wall read -25 degrees. It was closer to forty below at the line cabin. Never have I been so cold.

Fortunately, the weather warmed a little, we replaced the antifreeze (both for the truck and for us), ate a hot meal and headed back up the mountain.

A day of planning, story telling and consuming Kentucky's best outlasted the cold snap and for the next three days we tromped canyons, ridges and ledges looking for tracks in the ever deepening snow.

By the time we found a set of prints the weather was marginal, so we opted for survival rather than a successful hunt.

The trip back to Wichita was long and tedious as we dodged black ice patches and winter snow storms. We made it, or I wouldn't be telling this story. But, the real prize was the birth of a lifelong infatuation with the rugged wilderness, the thrill of the hunt and the uncanny feeling that I had done all this before. Maybe I had.

Mountain Lion Motivation

Scared - Lordy, was I scared! I've read of incidents where the adrenaline rush was so powerful one could lift a car off a person caught beneath it. I always took such stories with a grain of salt - until it happened to me.

I was attending University of Utah working on my Master's degree. My friend, Ed Connolly, was studying for his Master's in biology. His thesis involved the food habits and territorial range of the mountain lion, a program that involved 'hands on' activity in the field. Ed and his program advisor designed a study which required capturing as many lions as possible in an isolated mountain range near Ely, Nevada, ear tagging them and releasing them. As they would be trapped later, hopefully the ear tags would be returned to the University. Ed could then determine, from the capture point, the lion's range from the initial tagging point.

Doesn't that sound simple?

I had nothing to do with the study except that Ed needed help. In those days I was enthusiastic about anything to do with running around in the mountains so I volunteered.

We discussed devising a method of capturing the study animals with the least danger of being 'clawed or chawed' by somewhat furious mountain lions. The particular strain of felis concolor inhabiting the Central Rocky Mountains is the largest subspecies of the feline which ranges from Patagonia to Canada. Two hundred pound animals are the norm. A lion this size has the strength to kill a full grown elk or a yearling colt and drag it a quarter mile upslope to a secluded dining place in the rocks and ledges. They are powerful!

Ed had an idea. We would devise a tool which would allow a person to pin the animal down, once it had been chased into a tree by hounds. He could then step close and install an ear tag with minimum danger. Since we had to race after the hounds through ledges and up cliffs, it needed to be easily transportable and light enough to carry in a back pack. We took a 10-foot section of aluminum tubing, cut it into 30-inch lengths and collared them for quick assembly. Then we threaded an aircraft control cable through the pipe and fashioned a loop on the 'active' end. The other end was knotted so that, once the loop had been dropped over the lion's head, it could be pulled snug and the knot slipped into a locking notch at the top end. Sounds like a great idea, right?

But, we thought it should be tested before trying it in the field.

Ed had a working relationship with the Salt Lake City zoo, having delivered several mountain lion kittens to them captured earlier by government predator hunter buddies of his. The zoo planned to raise them to adulthood then trade them to other zoos in the world for their indigenous animals. It was a cheap way for the zoo to increase their animal inventory.

The zoo keeper in charge of large cats had a pair of half-grown lions nearly ready to trade. They weighed about 100 pounds each and, including their tails, were six feet long. The cage was twenty-four feet square and twelve feet high bolted onto a concrete slab. As we prepared to enter, the zoo keeper raised the sliding door and slipped into the enclosure. Ed and I followed his lead. Since it was Ed's study and he had the ear tag pliers, he and the zoo keeper would implant the tags. That left me to handle the snare.

We eased toward the frightened animals which stayed as far away from us as possible. Slowly I maneuvered the loop over the head of one as Ed kept him distracted. A quick yank on the cable and I slipped the knot into the retainer slot. All seemed to be going as planned. But, the lion, feeling the bite of the cable, squalled like a banshee and lunged away. His great strength was awesome. As he shook his head, bit the cable, rolled on the floor and leaped sideways, the pipe snapped at all four joints. I was tethered to an extremely upset lion on a free-swinging line.

I don't clearly remember the rapidly developing events that followed. But, as I hung on , the zoo keeper grabbed the lion's tail and we stret=====ched him out between us. All this time the other one was pacing frantically across the cage a short jump away. Ed eased in closer and, between head jerks and flailing paws, managed to clip a tag in one ear. The idea was to determine if it would stay or be scratched off by the cat. We decided to quit with one tag while we were ahead.

Then came the release procedure. Ed jumped back, the zoo keeper released his hold and I somehow managed to shake the loop loose all at the same time. Talk about action! Both cats circled the cage staying as far away from us as possible. We eased toward the door. The zoo keeper then reached outside and retrieved a can of warm salt water laced with medication. He was treating one of the lions for an eye infection. We didn't know this so, as he slowly moved across the cage, Ed quickly raised the gate, slipped out and dropped it back in place behind him. Then I prepared to do the same.

Just as I turned my back, the other lion raced away from the approaching zoo keeper. I reached for the door to make a quick exit. The same instant the racing lion brushed my legs as he lunged past. That's when I panicked. I thought I had been attacked. The lion was just in frantic retreat from the zoo keeper but the result was spectacular. I went straight up to the top of the twelve foot cage in one leap. You talk about an adrenaline surge! I don't remember ever touching the side of the cage on the way up. I simply shot up like a rocket. Ed was doubled over outside the cage at my aerial antics. He could see that the cat was just as scared as I was. And I was some kind of scared.

It was an easy thing to get out once the zoo keeper had splashed the salt water into the infected eyes and returned to my side of the cage. But, I'll long remember the feeling of that brush against my leg just knowing the next sensation would be teeth in my calf.

Scared? You better believe it!

Oh, the pipe tool? We discarded the idea.

Home, Sweet Home

"Y" Camp and the Parade of Homes happened the same week that year. It wouldn't have made any difference except for the circumstances which evolved. For my wife and me it was an inconvenience - for son, Dean, it was traumatic.

I had built an award winning home for the Parade. Its focal point was a garden room complete with pool and fountain. Beautiful green foliage in a flagstone planter hid the source of the water which flowed down a cantilevered stone projection then cascaded into a sparkling pool. Swimming goldfish added a splash of color. Green Vermont slate paved the floor. An eight foot sliding glass door opened to the fenced garden and a six foot slider accessed the dining room. Guests at the dining table could view the garden room as they ate.

An especially designed kitchen, raised hearth fireplace, slate front entry with a center knob on the door all added class. It should have been an award winner - and it was.

The best part of the situation happened when it sold in advance of the Parade and the buyer agreed to delay closing until after the Parade.

Coincidentally, Dean was scheduled to attend his very first YMCA summer resident camp 40 miles west of Colorado Springs in Eleven Mile Canyon. He was thrilled and a little scared at the same time. His eagerness was tempered by the thought of "cutting loose" some of the parental control strings. It was to be a great learning experience - even more than he could imagine at the time.

We drove him to camp with one of his buddies who was also a "first timer." His buddy's parents were to pick them up the following Saturday evening and bring them home.

You know the adage that begins, "The best laid plans.....?" They went awry again.

The Parade of Homes was a great success. Many, many people admired our 'award winner' - but bought the more traditional ones on the street. No problem. My house was sold - until Tuesday when the buyer failed to qualify for his loan. So, what do you do with an award winning home that didn't sell? We did the thing that seemed most logical at the time. We decided to move in.

On Thursday we contacted a mover and on Friday we moved. Just that quickly.

Since Dean wasn't due back from Camp until Saturday night, we spent Saturday morning getting settled in the new home. Our plan was to go over to the old house early in the evening and wait for Dean.

However, Camp let out early and Dean was dropped off at "home" about noon. He waved good bye to his friend and hauled his gear up to the front door. It was locked. He rang the door bell. No one came to the door. So, he went around to the back to look in the living room windows.

There was no furniture! Had his parents shipped him off to camp and then moved away leaving him stranded?

One can imagine the thoughts that raced through the head of that ten year old. He went back to the front and sat down on the steps to try to figure out what to do next. Then, a neighbor spotted him. She rushed out to him just before the tears began to flow. She explained the situation and called us.

Believe me, Dean was one happy camper when we drove up to take him to his new home. He's never taken anything for granted since.

Where's Daryl?

Son, Dean, is endowed with special awareness which provides him an unerring sense of direction under any circumstance. Son, Daryl, has many talents, but this isn't one of them.

In the mid-50's, when the boys were seven and nine, I used to take them into the mountains of the Front Range in Colorado in my battered jeep. I enjoyed teaching them to be perceptive of nature and at home in the woods. We would spot elusive game - mule deer, elk, and occasionally bighorn sheep. We identified tracks made in the mud or snow, differentiating the pointed, heart-shaped deer track from the more oval bighorn. They learned the coyote tracks always had toenail impressions while the bobcat track was more rounded and never showed claw marks.

As a training measure to prevent getting lost, we would drive the jeep off-road through the timber, uphill and down, twisting and reversing direction until we were 'lost'. Then I would ask,

"Which way is the road?"

Dean would inevitably point the correct direction. Daryl would just as consistently point another way. I would often park the jeep and we would hike through the dense woods a few hundred yards, turning and meandering to confuse direction. Then I would choose one or the other to lead us back to the jeep. Even if Daryl were pointed in the correct direction to start, he would soon be 90 degrees off course and I would have to realign him. Dean, on the other hand, would, without prompting, make a beeline for the jeep and find it with minimum effort.

Consequently, my instruction was naturally to say to Daryl when they were hiking,

"Stay with Dean and he'll show you the way home."

It usually worked, except for that eventful Sunday at the Divide, Colorado, cabin. The boys and their cousins, Johnny and Rob, were back at the far end of the property, perhaps a half mile away, climbing around in some rocks.

Dad and Mom had come out from Kansas on vacation. Brother John and his family were already there and we celebrated with a picnic. The cabin was located a mile back from the highway on 160 acres of timbered land southwest of the town of Divide. It was a great July day - lots of food, wonderfully cool mountain breezes, deep blue skies at that 9,000 foot elevation, and an awesome view of Pikes Peak.

The afternoon was winding down and everyone was making moves to clean up the 'leavings' and go home. The four boys had been gone two or three hours and, as evening approached, headed back to the cabin. They arrived excited and exhausted from their explorations. All except for Daryl.

"Where's Daryl?" someone asked.

"I don't know," Dean, the oldest of the four replied. "He was following us when we left the rocks."

I shouted his name. No response. "No worry," we said, "he'll straggle in." But, he didn't.

It was beginning to get dark before we really became concerned. A quick trip up the trail to the rocks and repeated yells evoked no response. So, we ran back and discussed a plan of action. Some would stay at the cabin. John and I would take separate cars to circle the area as best we could in the fading light. Dad and I circled out around to the west while John took the east direction. I found a pasture road a mile west that led up an open draw toward the back of our property. I cruised the rapidly diminishing trail honking the horn and yelling for Daryl. As the light faded the trail ended. I stopped before turning around. There was twenty miles of wilderness between us and the old mining town of Cripple Creek. That's a lot of area to get lost in.

Suddenly Dad exclaimed, "What's that up in the timber?"

We jumped out and ran toward a forlorn, disheveled boy who walked purposefully toward us. After hugs and grins I asked Daryl what happened.

"I must have taken a wrong turn when I left the rocks," he said. "I went back for my stick I left against a tree and lost sight of the guys. Then, Dad, when I realized I was lost, I remembered what you told me, 'Head downhill until you find a road and follow it.' And, here I am."

There was much joy and thanksgiving in the Prigmore family that night.

Speed Dumb

What's the fastest you ever drove a car - on the highway, not a race track? My speedometer read 125 miles per hour. Let me tell you about it - but, don't tell my grandkids.

The best car I ever owned was a 1955 Buick Roadmaster. It rode the easiest, drove the sweetest, looked the nicest and handled the best of any of my several Buicks. I bought it new in 1954. I've forgotten the price. But, it didn't matter anyway because I loved that car. It was a 'road' car, at its best on the highway floating along in solid control at 80, 85 or 90. I usually cruised in that range — those days of no speed limits and no interstate highways.

We were going home for Christmas from Colorado Springs to Kansas. It was traditional. Sometimes the weather was clear and beautiful; other times we skated on sleet or ice.

This day started out like any other travel day - pack the car, load the kids, check the oil and gas and hit the road. The day was clear and cold. We made good time through eastern Colorado and into western Kansas on state road 96. There's a 25-mile stretch of road between Scott City and Deighton, Kansas, that's straight as a string. It's a two-lane black top and there were very few cars on it. I had just passed a farm pickup and looked down the road ahead. Not a car in sight for two or three miles, so I didn't let up on the accelerator. I had always wanted to test the top speed of this wonderful car. Now seemed the optimum time.

If we had taken a democratic vote the family in the car, inluding my mother-in-law, would have outvoted me four to one - but, we didn't. I just put the pedal to the metal and we moved smoothly past 100 without effort. 110 was just as easy and the needle kept moving. At 120 I was having 'butterflies'. So, as it inched on up to 125, I was ready to back off.

I don't know if that was top speed for the Roadmaster - I *do* know it was top speed for *me* and *far past* the family's tolerance level. My 'folly' continued to be a prime topic of conversation the rest of the trip.

I was 'ego-centered' in those days and seldom failed to brag about my '125-mile-per-hour car' when the occasion presented itself.

The next fall I drove out to eastern Colorado to go Canada goose hunting with my brother-in-law, Jack Hagemen, and friends Bob Clark and Burr Roberts. Four of us had rolled out in the pre-dawn hours to go sit in a blind, hoping some geese would come to our decoys. They didn't. About 11 a.m. we gave up looking and headed to the house for lunch. After lunch, Jack suggested it was too early to go back out and that late afternoon would be a better hunting time. So, we took naps.

Nobody awakened us until nearly four p.m. and it was an hour's drive to the lake.

"Don't worry," I bragged, "We'll take the Roadmaster and cut our time by a third or more."

Again, the old 'best laid plans' adage kicked in.

I explained to the guys that, in order to get even more power from that V-8 engine, I had replaced the regulation spark plugs with some hot new items called 'fire injectors'. The four electrodes were supposed to add extra quick firing ability to give more 'OOMPH'.

We grabbed our guns, jumped into the Buick and hit the road. I was pushing 105 when there was a distinct 'ping' followed by a bang under the hood. My speed dropped rapidly and I slowly rolled to a stop. When I raised the hood I noticed the oil filler cap, which just pushed onto the filler tube, was gone. Jack ran back down the road and picked it up. No one had a clue why it had happened. I stuck it back on and started the engine. 'Bang'! It blew off again. Then we knew we had major motor troubles. Pressure in the crankcase strong enough to blow the filler cap off meant there was compression coming from a cylinder escaping into the crankcase.

Four days and $400 later a local mechanic had replaced a piston that had a dime-sized hole in the top. The 'fire injectors' had apparently injected too much *fire*.

After that the car never ran as smooth again. I guess the replacement piston wasn't exactly weight-matched because the engine vibrated above 70 mph.

So, I sold it and moved on to a 1956 red Buick convertible - but, that's another story

"I Got Kicked Out of Church"

I got kicked out of church - on Easter Sunday! Well, it wasn't really "church." It was Easter sunrise service in the Garden of the Gods near Colorado Springs. I was the kickee; the kicker was a horse, a skittish bay gelding unaccustomed to large crowds. People were scurrying like ants from a disturbed hill after the last "amen."

Here's what happened:

In the mid-60's we were living in Colorado Springs. My folks drove out from Kansas to spend the Easter weekend with us. One of the highlights was the sunrise service and pageant near the gateway rocks. A natural amphitheater provided an ideal setting to portray the Easter story complete with costumed disciples, Mary and the empty tomb. A narrator read the 28th chapter of Matthew as if he had written it himself. It was stirring and emotional as more than eight thousand worshippers immersed themselves in the never-old story.

Then it was over and, as in most church services, the crowd scattered like quail to their cars in order to escape the ubiquitous traffic jam. That is, most of them did. Some rode horseback from nearby stables intending to continue their trail ride after "church."

One of these was an inexperienced 13 year old girl. As people rushed by, her horse spooked and tried to escape the chaos. She valiantly hung onto the bridle reins as the gelding pulled back, swinging our way in an arc from the girl's pivot.

Dad and Mom were just getting up to shake out their

ground cloth. I spotted the approaching crisis and quickly stepped between them and the lethal end of the horse. I must have seemed a threat because, as his rump swung even with me, he humped his back and kicked me on the side of my thigh. Fortunately, he was close enough that he didn't get full extension or he might have broken my leg. As it was, I was shoved into Mom, knocking her down. I staggered along trying to regain my balance. I was 20 or 30 feet out of the amphitheater when I recovered my balance; hence, I was "kicked out of church."

We took Mom to the emergency room for a check-up. She was fine. But, over the next few days and weeks I sported the worst looking bruises you could imagine. The healing process slowly worked the discoloration down my leg until my entire foot was a blue-black-greenish mottled mess. Eventually it dissipated, but I'll forever see in slow motion that unexpected benediction to a very singular spiritual experience.

Jim Beam

One April day, Ed Connolly called from Boise and said the steelhead were running. I didn't know what that meant until Ed explained that steelhead trout, a cousin to rainbow, hatched, migrated to the ocean, lived there and grew big for three years, then swam back up the same rivers and streams to the point of their hatching. On the way up we could catch some whoppers. I'd never fished for steelhead, but when Ed said the spawners weighed from 15 to 30 pounds, I was ready.

A call to "Robin" (Dr. Robert Clark, DVM) in Kansas City, the third member of our "war-time-buddy" trio, got an enthusiastic response.

"Hell yes, I'll go! When do we leave?" was his enthusiastic response.

I lived in Colorado Springs at the time and Bob had a veterinary practice in Kansas City, a small animal hospital. He flew to Denver where I joined him. Then we flew Frontier Airlines to Salt Lake City and on to Boise.

An overnight with Ed and Louise gave us time to assemble gear and plan our trip into the Middle Fork of the Salmon River wilderness area.

Ed was a "revenuer," an agent for the U.S. Alcohol and Tobacco Tax Unit of the Internal Revenue Service. His job was to ferret out moonshiners in the wilder areas of Idaho and Montana, plan raids, make the "busts," arrest the illegal distillers and collect enough evidence to prosecute. Sometimes the "evidence" was in whiskey bottles collected from bars and garbage dumps - Jim Beam, Southern Comfort, Wild Turkey and especially vodka bottles. The 190 proof moonshine was crystal clear and potent. Some of the producers came from the hills of West Virginia and Tennessee where whiskey making was a family craft for two hundred years. They knew their stills.

Ed was a very thorough and detailed investigator. He left nothing to chance. Most of his cases ended in convictions. Part of his "backup" evidence was stored away from the courthouse for safety.

It just "happened" this particular morning that a stray bottle was "stored" with our fishing gear as we drove north to Riggins, then back onto a gravel road along the Middle Fork toward Yellow Pine. We had fished several holes unsuccessfully and were standing by the pickup sampling Ed's "evidence" when around the corner came an Idaho Fish and Game truck. The driver stopped to visit his old friend, Ed, with whom he had shared many a campfire.

"Hi, Fred. Catchin' any poachers?," Ed inquired.

"Naw," replied Fred, "How's fishing?'

"About as good as catchin' poachers, I guess," Ed responded. "How about a drink?"

"Don't mind if I do," grinned Fred. He was not unaware of Ed's job.

Ed reached into the pickup and lifted out the Jim Beam bottle. Fred took it, glanced at the label and tilted it to his lips. A couple of swallows later he pulled it back down wheezing and coughing. Tears misted his eyes as he looked at the label again and whispered through a tortured throat, "Best damn Jim Beam I ever tasted!"

Brummie

'Brummie' Brumbaugh was a Clear Creek County (Colorado) legend. He was one of the last of the Old West sheriffs who took no guff from anybody - not politicians, not do-gooders, not city-slick attorneys nor smart-ass kids. He wrote the script and starred in the action. His 'Presence' was Law.

I came to know Brummie through my partner, Ellis Lupton, who was a 'mover and shaker' in back room politics. He had done some favors for Brummie over the years. I was a home builder planning to develop a subdivision in Georgetown on Ellis' land. We 'hired' Brummie to protect our building materials and construction in his 'off duty' hours. He, in turn, commissioned me a Deputy Sheriff. I still have the badge. (It figures prominently in the "Flight to Africa" story.)

There were many who didn't like Brummie because he 'stepped on their bubble gum'. He couldn't be bribed nor intimidated. Rough as a cob and ornery as a sidewinder when crossed, he was, none-the-less, honest and absolutely fear-less. Never mind that he drank a quart of Seagram 7 every day; ignore the fact that he somewhat intimidated opposition; don't bother to try to keep track of him and his activities; the important thing was, no Colorado county had less crime than Clear Creek while Brummie was sheriff.

Brummie thought the world of Jeni. He gave us the key to his 'retreat' home in Empire, Colorado, so we would have a place to vacation in the mountains. He insisted we use the steaks from the freezer, booze from the well stocked bar and food from the pantry. When Brummie's day at the office was done, although he lived on 24-hour ready alert, he would stop by the cabin and visit awhile. One night he came in while I was playing the piano. He was ecstatic.

"Let's liven up the joint," he said. So, he went to the closet, pulled out a big bass fiddle and we had a jam session. Jeni sang some but laughed more as I banged out "Saints," "Beer Barrel Polka" and other tunes while Brummie slapped that bass. At times he would straddle it like a stock pony and never miss a beat. I think it was one of the few times in his life he could really let his hair down without fear of criticism. He knew he was among friends. As much as he drank, I never saw Brummie drunk - or even less than in full control.

One Sunday night in January, several hot-shot young skiers were returning to Denver from Vail and 'feeling their oats'. They breezed into the only bar in Georgetown open at that hour and proceeded to get rowdy and intoxicated. A 911 call went out for Brummie. The dispatcher quickly located him and briefed the situation. A few minutes later Brummie walked in and took command.

"Al right, boys," he said, "You've had your fun. Now it's time to call it an evening. Go on home. Your parents are probably worried about you."

"Ha!," shouted one belligerent kid. "Who does this old man think he is, telling us what to do? Let's take his gun and tie him up."

In a flash, 'quick-draw-Brummie' drew, not his gun, but his MACE cylinder from its belt holster. As they charged him he cut loose a cloud of pepper MACE that stopped them cold. It laid them out flat on the floor. Then he handcuffed them, hauled them off to jail, checked their ID's and called their parents.

When the parents offered to come right up and get them, Brummie said, "Don't bother me tonight. I'm going back to bed. Come get them in the morning. It'll do them good to spend a night in jail."

Believe me, when Brummie said, "Sit down," people sat; and when Brummie said, "Stand up," you'd better get on your feet. When Brummie said, "Don't cause problems in my county," residents and visitors listened and believed!

I have a "feather mattress" theology. Most people like their theology firm. Mine supports me, enfolds me, comforts me. Others may punch at it but they meet no resistance. My "feather mattress" theology absorbs life with non-judgment and unconditional love.

Wolf Creek Pass

The Cessna 170 was under powered for mountain flying. I was 'under houred' as a pilot for mountain flying. The combination almost caused a disaster.

I had taken off from Peterson Field near Colorado Springs at dawn and headed southwest past the shoulder of Pikes Peak before turning west through LaVeta Pass. The Great Sand Dunes slipped by beneath my aluminum wings. Artesian wells spouted life-giving water into San Luis Valley, turning the desert into an oasis.

I was headed into Wolf Creek Pass in southwest Colorado at 13,000 Feet, easily high enough to clear the terrain ahead. The Pass was only 10,800, but mountains towered into the four-teens both north and south of me as I flew a heading of 210 degrees toward Pagosa Springs. My destination was Cortez, in the shadow of Mesa Verde, where Anasazi cliff dwellings had gathered dust for a thousand years. My years ahead suddenly appeared abbreviated as I met one of Nature's idiosyncrasies.

The weather was clear. I had checked before leaving Colorado Springs two hours earlier. If it had been otherwise I would never have taken off. You just don't fly VFR (visual flight regulations) in the mountains in bad weather. Normally friendly cumulus clouds sometimes turn into granite-cumulus with hard rock centers in the mountains. There's a saying I learned my first day of flight school: 'There are old pilots and there are bold pilots, but there are no old, bold pilots. I'm a fair weather flyer.

Suddenly, about five miles from the Pass, I began to lose

altitude - rapidly! I increased power to the firewall and still plunged earthward. 12,500 - 12,000 - 11,500 - 11,000 and wolf Creek Pass began to climb above my line of flight. I rapidly scoured my limited meteorological memory library and remembered that the jet stream always flowed west-to-east across the U. S. It sometimes blew at 200 miles per hour or more. As it hit the western slope of the continental divide and surged upward, it created an airfoil. When it cleared the summit it curled downward pressing like a giant hand on my airplane. Its power was awesome. I could turn back and abort the mission. But, I really needed to be in Cortez where I had a building project going. Several closings were scheduled and my banker was expecting me. Decision time!

All this time, only seconds, although it seemed much longer, thoughts pro and con flashed through my head. Wolf Creek Pass drew closer and closer. I still had space to do a 180, even though timbered slopes were rapidly funneling me towards the gap. Just about the time I decided to turn back my altimeter, reading less than 10,000 feet, began to wind back up. I cut power and still shot upward like an elevator. I reasoned that the jet stream, compressed at the summit, had curled over and down in a wave. Most of the wind continued eastward, but enough curled under to lift me like a feather. Through 11,000 feet, then 12,000, I sailed over Wolf Creek Pass at 13,000 feet before hitting the wall of air from the southwest. Luckily it wasn't moving at 200 mph at my altitude or I would have been flying backward. On the west side of Wolf Creek the terrain falls off rapidly so I was able to power my way down to a lower elevation where I could pick up some ground speed.

Keep in mind, this was in the 50's and we didn't have sophisticated navigational aids to keep us on track through the mountains. I was out of range of every OMNI station and radio frequency. My flight plan stated I would be in Cortez three hours after takeoff. No way was I going to make it - nor was my fuel supply sufficient.

As I approached Durango I called the airport tower and requested a straight-in approach to the runway on Florida Mesa. It was approved and I touched down with a sigh of relief. I called the bank in Cortez, refueled and quickly flew the last fifty miles, only an hour or so late for the closings. But, I was on terra firma in good health, not on the side of a mountain in a pile of airplane wreckage.

Going home was another adventure.

Make compost of the crap in your life!

Wide-awake

If there ever was a misnomer for a surplus army mule it was my Shrine Unit mount, Wide-awake. In the mid-50's I completed my consistory work and became a 32 degree Mason. I was then eligible to join the "fun" club of the Masonic Order, the Shriners, which I proceeded to do.

Most Shrine Clubs, whose primary purpose is to support Children's Hospitals, are most well known for their special parade units. In every parade from small town to metropolis Shriners ride highly decorated motorcycles, horses, motor-bikes, midget cars or such with their distinctive adornment. It's fun time for adult kids. Each club strives to outdo its rival clubs for uniqueness and style.

When the army high command decided to dismantle their last "mule-fueled" mountain artillery division at Ft. Carson, Colorado, they auctioned off surplus mules. Our club hit upon the idea of a parade unit of Shriner mounted mules. As one guy chortled,

"Now we can really make asses of ourselves."

No one else in the country had such a unit. We could be unique.

My problem was, where would I keep Wide-awake, my special purchase? The neighbors in town would object, I was sure, to a dawn-announcing mule braying at the sunrise. Fortunately, a rancher friend south of town agreed to board him for $30 per month. A dollar a day for an animal that would only be ridden a few times a year? Who's the jackass here, you ask?

Well it seemed worthwhile at the time. The Pike's Peak Range Ride was coming up and I planned a "rocking chair" ride on Wide-awake. A mule is easy on the backside, particularly for one who only rides occasionally. Bring on the 125-mile ride. I was prepared.

The trouble was, mules are smarter than horses. Wide-awake disliked the preparations - fitting the saddle cinch, adjusting the breaching, tying on the saddle bags and slicker - so he vanished the day before the street breakfast that celebrated the beginning of the ride. It was only then I discovered he could walk up to a six foot fence and leap over it. I found out later from the army that he did that with regularity before maneuvers. The surplus description didn't list that nasty habit when they advertised him.

Fortunately, a neighboring rancher, on his way to town spotted Wide-awake heading for Mexico. He hazed him into a barn where I retrieved him and haltered him in a box stall until the ride.

He performed well on the ride, except he was difficult to mount. The big critter stood 16 hands and had legs like a giraffe. I often wished I could have raced him.

I struggled through the Autumn with that unpredictable beast. Hardly a week went by that I didn't get a call from the rancher.

"Wide-awake's gone again," he'd say, "Better come help me find him." And the calls never came at an opportune time.

So, election day came and went and plans were made to inaugurate a new president. Our Shrine Unit was invited to ride in the Inaugural Parade. I couldn't get away from my business. So, reluctantly, I sold Wide-awake to another Shriner who did ride him down Pennsylvania Avenue in pomp and style. If I know Wide-awake he probably expressed his opinion of politics and politicians with piles in the street.

With mixed feelings I closed the book on Wide-awake.

Flight to London

Hour after hour the soft drone of the giant Rolls Royce engines caressed my subconscious as I dozed fitfully in the night, at times dimly aware of the great speed of the VC-10 hurling me toward London.

Suddenly, wide awake by a startling discovery of natural light, I felt the soft symphony of dawn breaking over the fantasia of multi-level clouds and azure sky. The high and haughty cirrus were the first to reflect the glow of the approaching sun. Their cold blue iciness began to melt into delicate pastels of sunrise. At once lavender, then pink, and almost immediately rose, the breaking day gained momentum. In a flash the wing tip was painted orange as if re-entry had heated it to a glow.

Rapidly, the night faded behind as the morning reached downward toward the steel gray Atlantic far below. The isolated mountain peaks of cumulus became aglow as their pseudo-snow caps were touched by the brush of the Master artist at work this new day.

Then, as the Irish coast pushed itself from the Eastern sea, an undulating carpet of low stratus blanketed the landscape, as if tucked about the neck of a sleepy child.

It was while absorbing the unspeakable beauties of this experience that I felt the warmth begin to fade. We were coasting downhill toward London on a collision course with the ominous fog bank, its chilling shroud enveloping us in a disoriented nothingness of non-color.

Longingly, my eyes reached back for a last glimpse of the priceless Rembrandt painted on the disappearing canvas. It was gone; gone, leaving only the image, alive and indelible on my mind.

The subconscious mind is the alchemist that transmutes energy into actuality.

Nairobi

How many of us write down our dreams and aspirations at 10 or 12 years of age? Most of us do not. But, I can vividly remember dreaming of going on safari in Africa when I was that age. Nairobi was as real to me as Wichita. I devoured geography and Africa was the great unknown 'dark continent' full of mystery and intrigue.

Perhaps it was in my genes to explore. I was born into a generation once removed from pioneers. Dad moved to Kansas from Tennessee at age six in a wagon. He remembered crossing the Mississippi on a flatboat. One of his great uncles traveled with Daniel Boone from Kentucky, when it became too crowded there, to central Missouri. There are still a good many Prigmore's in Boone and Blackwater counties. Earlier, my multiple great-grandfather floated down the Tennessee River on a flatboat to 'walk off' a tract of land in the Sequatchie River valley near Chattanooga in the 1790's.

Hunting and fishing was a way of life that spilled over into my early years. I bought a single shot .22 caliber rifle when I was 13 with the first money I earned away from home. I remember it cost $3.50 from a mail order catalog - Stoeger's, I think. I still look at that gun and remember how ecstatic I was when I opened the box. Crown jewels couldn't have excited me more. Guns for hunting were common then. Every farmer used them to 'harvest' rabbits, squirrels and quail to supplement the family groceries.

So, it was not unusual that I dreamed of greater hunts,

bigger game, the ultimate challenge for my budding interest in big game. I can remember making a list of the items I would need for my envisioned trip to Nairobi and into the bush. I listed a tent, sleeping bag, mosquito net, canteen, thorn-proof clothes, snake-proof boots, a wide brim 'safari' hat and other items more numerous than practical, I'm sure.

But, most important, I needed a rifle suitable for elephant, cape buffalo, rhino and lions. I poured over the Stoeger catalog for hours, studying ballistics, muzzle velocities, shock energy at 100 and 200 yards and effective range. I settled on a Wembley .600 nitro express. It seemed to have it all. I could see myself fearlessly facing a charging cape buffalo and dropping him to a sliding finish merely inches from my smoking gun. It was REAL for me. I'm sure Mom or Dad would rather I cleaned my room or picked potato bugs in the garden.

Thirty years later my dream became a reality, adjusted only by my substitution of a camera for a rifle.

It was in the late-1960's when the opportunity came for me to 'invade' Africa. I was manufacturing a 110-volt automotive generator under the name, 'Mobilectric', and found the opportunity to open a market in South Africa. I flew from Denver to New York where I embarked on a BOAC flight to London, Geneva and Africa. I was filled with bubbling anticipation of establishing a distributor for my product and then, somehow, getting into the bush.

After a long flight, I landed in Johannesburg (Joburg in local terms). A call to Pretoria, a few miles to the north, brought an 'air taxi' to pick me up. At Wunderboom Airport I met my host and, hopefully, new distributor. Peter Von der Wooda owned the Piper Aircraft franchise for the thirteen countries south of the equator. He also owned thousands of acres in the lower veldt beyond the Drakensberg Mountains. He told me the story of how he acquired so much land for so little money:

After World War II, he bought a dozen or so war surplus Lancaster bombers for 'scrap'. There was motive in his madness, however. He planned to purchase land in the lower veldt which couldn't be used for agriculture due to the infestation of the tsetse fly which no one had been able to eradicate. The fly, which infected cattle with a fatal disease, was highly mobile and couldn't be sprayed locally because they simply flew a few hundred feet and escaped the spray. Peter repaired the Lancasters and fitted spray tanks in the bomb bays with spray jets wing tip to wing tip. After his land purchase, which most people considered 'Peter's folly', he embarked on an eradication program. He scraped off a landing strip, hauled in thousands of gallons of spray from Durban, flagged the boundaries of his land and hired pilots. He then flew the Lancasters, which he had renovated, wing tip to wing tip in a line a quarter mile wide, boundary to boundary. The flies couldn't escape and were eradicated. He could then bring in cattle without the disease problem. It worked and he became rich.

So, after our business was concluded, he invited me to his boma (home in the bush) for the weekend. To avoid a business-ending catastrophe, he and his son, who was operations manager, never flew in the same plane. Consequently, we took two planes from his inventory and flew from Pretoria to his farm. His staff of blacks included a housekeeper, cook, game tracker and others. They were well-treated and, usually, were on the job with efficiency and capability. However, if one of them failed to meet expectations, they heard about it in spades! The real power in Peter's operation was Zingy Harrison, a WW II Spitfire pilot, soldier of fortune, and right hand man. He managed everything, the farm, the Piper agency, other businesses and Peter's 'surreptitious foreign affairs'. He was the enforcer the staff feared.

Zingy grew up with the Bantu because his father was a game management official of some kind out in the bush. He could cuss in all the dialects south of Timbuktu and consequently command the attention of the native staff. When Zingy yelled, "JUMP", the only question was, "how high?"

A short dirt strip had been scraped out of the bush on a flat area along the Olifant River. We buzzed the field first to clear off a small herd of elephants grazing on acacia trees. Then we made the final approach on power, ready to abort if game reoccupied the landing strip. They didn't. We touched down and rolled to a stop. The British 'combie' (an extended cab pickup) pulled up to transport us to the house. Zingy left a couple of staff people at the plane to discourage curious animals.

The ranch house was unlike any Zane Grey western. It was shaped like a dumbbell with the kitchen and eating area in one round unit. At the other end of an open stone veranda was the sleeping rhounduval.

At the front of the building overlooking the river was a large patio area surrounded by a low stone wall with a fire pit in the center. As it began to grow dark, we adjourned from the sumptuous meal to lounge chairs under the southern cross. We were served South African brewed brandy that was as good as any I had ever tasted.

As I watched the unbelievable array of stars, one seemed to be moving. We came to the conclusion it was a satellite on course from Tenerife toward Australia.

Then, when it became fully dark, Peter said, "Do you want to hear some 'jungle music'?"

Naturally, I wanted to experience it all. So, he had a Bantu light the teepee-like stack of poles in the fire pit. Fire is nature's enemy. We certainly got a demonstration that night. As the flames leaped higher and higher the hippos in the Olifant River 300 yards away began to bellow. Then bull crocodiles added to the chorus. Lions roared, elephants trumpeted. It was truly a cacophony of wild and eerie 'music'.

I gloried in the realization that, here I was, living out my youthful fantasy in a very dramatic way. What an experience!

Grenada

I had never heard of Grenada until I was introduced to Premier Eric Gairy at a State party in the Bahamas. Lyndon Pindling, Bahamas' new premier, held a "thank you" extravaganza in Nassau honoring those instrumental in his election. I was not involved but Michael McLaney, who had asked Ellis Lupton and I to take charge of a development program he planned on Grand Bahama, was. We were evaluating the possibilities, and, while there, included in the guest list.

Mr. Gairy was desirous of establishing a national banking system for Grenada and had sought help from his friend, Premier Pindling. The timing was perfect. We were but a few steps away, near the punch bowl, when Mr. Pindling responded,

"Here are the persons you need to consult. Mr. Lupton and Mr. Prigmore. They are helping me develop our country."

Premier Gairy asked us to come down and talk to his key people. We agreed on a date a couple of weeks hence and planned our strategy. It was hinted we would be in a natural position to profit as agents for the government's substantial purchases of heavy construction equipment, aircraft, industrial equipment and other unspecified items. With dollar signs in our eyes we flew to Grenada via San Juan, Antigua and Barbados. One must overnight either in Barbados or Trinidad to catch the morning flight to Grenada's airport at Grenville, across the island from the capital, St. George's.

When we entered the terminal we were greeted by the Premier's driver with a limousine for the hour-long trip. We, being curious tourists, were intrigued by the banana groves, the nutmeg harvest, the mace drying, the women pounding clothes on rocks in the streams to wash them, and Grand Etang, the 4,000 foot extinct volcano towering over the island. We frequently requested the driver to stop so we could take photos. He seemed more and more disturbed and nervous with each stop. We discovered the reason when we were driven to the Premier's mansion to meet 18 cabinet members and ministers. They had been waiting for two hours while we were sightseeing!

We spent several days planning the Grenada National Bank and Trust Company with Ellis and I as two of the Directors. We hired a vice-president from Bank of Denver to come down on a two year contract to organize, train staff and operate the bank. We each invested $10,000 and helped raise a couple of hundred thousand more to capitalize it.

I thought, this was a super opportunity to make mega bucks in the international marketplace. Boy, was I *naive*! I didn't realize the intrigue and fancy footwork that occurs in international finance. It was a revelation for a Kansas farm boy who was raised to believe two and two always added up to four.

For instance: I got a call from someone wishing to borrow $100,000 from the Bank. They wished to secure the loan with certificates of deposit for a million dollars issued by the Bank of Sark, Channel Islands, UK.

It sounded like a good loan (at 18%) until I decided to call the Bank of Sark to verify the CD's. I asked to speak to the president when I finally got through at four a.m. (10 a.m. Sark time).

The sweet young voice informed me no was there but her and, when I questioned when I could speak to someone in authority, she had no idea when that could happen. Immediately a red flag began waving in my mind and, when she said she couldn't tell me any more about names of bank officers I closed the book on the deal.

Later, the Bank of Sark was exposed as a part of an international money scheme and I had just gotten a slight smell. It stunk.

We spent many days, Ellis and I, dealing with various ministers and agents, building a "want" list of major items. Our expectations soared, especially when the Premier would show up at our hotel nearly every evening for a few drinks and off color stories (He usually was accompanied by a sweet young "assistant.")

That was the high point of our Grenada project. As the months went by and our not-so-inexpensive trips added up, sans progress, relations deteriorated. It seemed no one could issue a purchase order on which to base an acquisition program. Our heavy equipment suppliers, whom we brought with us, gave up and went home. We became more and more discouraged even when Jeni and Lee (Ellis' wife) came to visit.

Finally, after months of trips back and forth, an incident at the bank nailed the coffin lid on our Grenada project. For some reason, the Bank Operating Manager, whom we recommended for the position, planned a trip to the States. On the morning he left, the bank was "robbed." An early arrival Bank employee found the vault door open and $5000 missing. No one was ever accused or caught but there was bad feeling.

So, we sold out and left the island with our investment intact but a ton of expense money and time down the tube.

So much for my banking career.

Flight to Africa

Fred eased the throttle forward to the stops. The twin turbo Lycomings revved to red line as the flat pitched props bit screaming slices from the humid air. The sluggish, overloaded Piper Navajo slowly gained speed. It rolled past the marker telling us there was seven thousand feet of the 11,000 foot runway remaining. Then we passed the six thousand marker and at five she was still well below flight speed. Would she reach rotation speed in the mile we had left of runway 9L at Miami International Airport? I wondered, as my inexperienced eyes danced across the instruments. At three thousand feet she began to feel lighter. We were 30% above the designed maximum gross weight, all of it fuel, in two aluminum tanks that filled the passenger cabin. It was an explosive capsule hovering on the edge of catastrophe. One skip of an engine, one blown tire, an erratic wind gust and we would end this delivery to South Africa in a ball of flame.

At fifteen hundred Fred eased her off and jerked the gear. We were flying, low and slow, but we *were* flying. I exhaled a great breath and wheezed, "That was a close one."

"Piece of cake," Fred grinned as we climbed through a thousand feet over Miami, two thousand over Miami Beach on a heading of 060 degrees. Next stop, Bermuda.

I thought back to the circumstances that evolved into the greatest adventure of my life. All my boyhood I dreamed of great adventures. I would climb the highest mountains; I would dive to ocean reefs alive with barracuda, sand sharks and millions of brilliantly colored fish; I would face a charging lion; I would fly my own plane across the ocean.

This trip was to check off two of those four dreams. We were actually flying the Atlantic. The lion incident came later in the trip.

The deep blue of the Bahamas trench changed to turquoise as Grand Bahama emerged from the horizon. Shallow coral reefs painted a tapestry of blues and greens. We droned on into the morning and three hours later Bermuda popped into view like a wart on the ocean surface. It was an easy first leg.

As I monitored the refueling and picked up the sandwiches for lunch, Fred checked the weather. Winds had picked up from the northeast and were just off the nose of our proposed route to the Azores. Our 14-hour fuel supply would give us only a 45 minute reserve if we went straight across.

"Not enough," wisely counseled the chief pilot, "We need to dogleg to Gander, Newfoundland."

"But, Gander's north," I observed. "Isn't that a long way out of the way?"

"Not so much," Fred explained, "If you look at a globe you'll see the 'great circle' route is not that much farther. It is usually the best way because of better prevailing winds."

So, refueled and well fed, we headed northeast for Newfoundland. As we cruised along at 13,000 feet on auto pilot, Fred and I dug out the cards to play gin rummy. Between Miami and Pretoria we played 180 games of gin. The main reason I won more than he did was his constant monitoring of the instrument panel and radio. Fred was a careful pilot.

The sun disappeared into the sea behind us and the sky ahead turned dark and ominous. With the cockpit lights on so we could see the spots on the cards, we dispelled the gloom.

Suddenly, there was a crack as something hit the windshield. Instantly alert, Fred's eyes roamed the panel. All gauges appeared normal. Then it happened again, a loud crack from outside.

"Oh, s___!," Fred exploded, "We're picking up ice."

I could see us riding an already overloaded plane into the freezing North Atlantic with survival chances about the same as the proverbial snowball in hell.

"Let's drop down into warmer air," I observed, "Maybe it will melt off." It sounded right to my limited experience with these conditions.

"Wrong," Fred corrected me, as he flipped on the landing lights to verify the ice buildup on wings and props. "Too many inexperienced pilots have thought that," he cautioned, "and as they drop lower and lower, the ice builds up faster and faster until there's no way to stop the descent. It's a sure way into the drink. We'll try to climb above the clouds into clear air. It will be colder, but it should stop the icing."

We added power and climbed through 14,000. We were still in the soup. At 15,000 it seemed brighter. As Fred was putting on his oxygen mask we broke out into the clear at 16,000 feet. The moon illuminated the clouds below like a fluffy carpet. Just as Fred had predicted, the rime ice stopped its buildup and began to flake off the props. Again, the chunks began to hit the windshield and outer skin as they left the spinning blades. But, now we didn't mind because it wasn't reforming as it flaked off.

Along about 10:30 the lights of coastal communities began to appear over the nose. Soon we were on a long final into Gander and, we hoped, a good night's rest. It was not to be.

As I again monitored the refueling process, Fred went in to close our flight plan and check the weather.

"Bad news," he reported upon his return. "They tell me we must leave in the next two hours or be stuck here for four days. There's a severe winter storm approaching."

We had a delivery schedule so there was no option. We must go. A quick meal in the airport beanery and we climbed aboard. This takeoff would be tricky and dangerous. It was eighteen degrees below zero with sheets of black ice on the runway. We lumbered onto the taxi way like a stuffed duck and Fred did the runup check. All appeared to be 'in the green'. Fortunately there wasn't a cross wind so we slowly accelerated toward rotation speed. It was 'heart-in-the-throat' time until we cleared the surface, tucked the gear and passed over the end of the strip.

Ten minutes out over the black water below, climbing slowly toward our assigned altitude, Fred radioed the local controller we were on our way. It was a little after midnight and we had been flying since nine a.m.

"Oh, by the way," the local told us, "Be on the lookout for sign of a Beech Bonanza. He left two days ago on your same heading and destination but hasn't been heard from since."

Great! I thought. Just what we needed to give us confidence on this nine-hour leg. Our only contact would be the periodic radio reports Fred would make to the Overseas Airways Controller each time we crossed an imaginary grid line on our flight path. The procedure operated, explained Fred, on the principle that if you missed two reports on your approved flight plan, Overseas Control alerted all ships and planes in your general area that you were 'unreported'. After three missed reports they pulled all stops and turned loose the Search and Rescue operation. We studiously checked time, airspeed, winds aloft and altitude in order to keep ourselves located on the Controller's map.

Moving southeast at 220 knots the sun literally lunged out of the horizon dead ahead. A red carpet unrolled before us on the choppy waters below. Onward we droned into the day, eagerly searching the horizon for the first glimpse of the Azores. To pass the time we played game after game of gin.

Suddenly, both engines coughed and quit!

"Damn!" breathed Fred. "We forgot to switch tanks."

Quickly but surely he moved the selector from the reserve tanks in the cabin, which were exhausted, to the wing tanks. Then, he switched on the booster pumps, set the mixture and throttle levers for 'start', and pressed the starter. A lifetime and five seconds later the left engine caught and roared into life. The right engine quickly followed. Again, I thanked my lucky stars that Fred was such a professional. He moved without the panic I felt and wasted no motion assessing the problem and rectifying it. Whew!

At last, Santa Maria sorted itself out of the widely scattered group of islands and we let down for a straight in approach. Touchdown, twenty-two hours out of Miami and time for a much needed rest in the local hotel. It wasn't the Hilton, but neither of us cared.

A few hours later, rested and refreshed, we ground checked the Navajo and topped the tanks. Next stop, Dakar in Senegal, the westerly most point in Africa, with the Atlantic to the west and the Sahara desert to the east. I visualized a second night over the ocean as we departed about nine p.m. Again, we climbed to our assigned altitude and pulled out the cards for more gin rummy. Periodically Fred radioed our position until one call was not answered. With some concern he checked several frequencies without success and concluded we had lost our long range broadcast capability. He continued to fiddle with it through the first check point, then the second.

"If I don't get some response soon," Fred worried, "They'll start to look for us."

As a last resort he flipped on his local transmitter to call for any planes or ships in the area. After the third or fourth 'send', the receiver crackled and a booming voice announced,

"Hello, little brother. This is KLM big brother overhead. How can we help you?"

Rapidly Fred outlined our problem and gave our last two position checks for relay to Overseas Control. We were off the hook and no more reports would be expected until we closed our flight plan upon reaching Dakar.

The Dakar strip was rough, which didn't seem to be a

problem on touchdown and roll out. But, takeoff with full tanks might pose a challenge. Fred replaced a transistor in the radio from his repair kit and we processed the official stuff that always accompanies foreign landings. It wouldn't be this easy at our next stop!

Local wisdom was to forget the 500 feet of runway at each end. It was the roughest. Start at 500, lock the brakes, run up power and kick it loose. We leaped forward building speed slowly. The roar from the coarse textured runway crescendoed as we accelerated. Just when I figured the tires might blow we cleared the ground. Whew! 'Another exciting adventure' it says in the travel brochure. Sure!

Our flight plan called for us to fly off shore in international airspace around the shoulder of Africa, past Liberia, Ivory Coast and Ghana. We would terminate in Lomé, Togo, where we would R.O.N. (remain overnight). Lomé was known in the international community as an easy transit refueling stop. That's if you stop, refuel and go. We didn't. And, that set the stage for a very scary situation.

The reason for the caution and careful planning was explained to me. Our ultimate destination, South Africa, was dramatically out of favor with all countries north of it due to its apartheid policy. This was in 1968. If any official at Dakar or Lomé or Luanda, our next stop, suspected we were going to deliver that Nav in Pretoria it would have been confiscated and we would have been locked up. Our *official* papers indicated we were terminating in Angola.

Fred, cautious but eager to get to Lomé, climbed only 2,500 feet out of Dakar before turning south. At Bissau, with no radar exposing our change in route, we turned inland. It would be three hours shorter - if we made it. Not only did we not have official clearance to overfly Guinea, Ivory Coast and Ghana, we would be over impenetrable jungle and crocodile filled rivers. In an emergency there was no safe place at all to set her down. Believe me, we breathed a huge sigh of relief when the Lomé

Airport appeared over the nose. This time we would get a good night's sleep and a hot meal.

We parked the plane in a transient area as directed and locked it up. Taking only our overnight bags, we cleared customs and caught the only taxi into town. Had we been Catholic we would have crossed ourselves before climbing into the decrepit antique. As it was, we looked at each other, shrugged our shoulders and said, "What the hell, we've no other choice."

The hotel was acceptable, the beds were tolerable and the food was palatable. So, we were in good spirits the next morning — that is, until we reached the airport. We paid the same taxi driver, grabbed our bags and went into the terminal.

Facing us was a 'welcoming committee' led by a very officious gentleman bedecked in proper attire, including morning coat with tails, striped pants and spats. At his right shoulder was a military person of obvious high rank with a left breastplate of ribbons and medals. Four armed enlisted men provided the 'muscle' should it be needed.

"We're in trouble," Fred whispered. "Let's see what they want."

"Good morning," announced Mr. Pompous, "I would like to visit your aircraft." His English was halting but understandable. Togo is a French speaking country, having once been a French colony.

"Fine," Fred agreed, "Rick, you show the gentleman the cockpit and preflight it. I'll settle up and be right out."

Now, I'm really naive. I thought he wanted to visit our brand new Piper Navajo to see if he liked it before ordering one. I gave him a great sales pitch. You'd have thought I was a factory rep. I squeezed him into the cockpit, went through the preflight check with him, checked clearances and started the engines. Everything checked out so I escorted him back outside thinking I had provided him a wonderful and informative 'visit'. He seemed quite perplexed and was seeking for more definitive words.

"I want to *inspect* the aircraft," he finally announced. I realized we were in big trouble if he found anything indicating we were delivering the plane to South Africa. I didn't know what we had aboard that might betray us. So, I countered with,

"I'm not authorized to permit that, sir. You'll have to discuss that with the Captain. Here he comes now."

"Fred," I related, "He wants to inspect the aircraft."

I had never seen Fred any way but serene, confident, assured and calm. But, he came unglued.

"INSPECT?" he shouted, "this aircraft is in transit and, according to international law, not subject to search. You have no right to demand such action."

I was sweating because it appeared Fred was talking us into bigger trouble. He argued and shouted, but the 'Mr. Big' was adamant. He must 'inspect' the aircraft.

I don't know what prompted me to do it, but I pulled out my wallet which had my gold, personalized deputy sheriff's badge from Clear Creek County, Colorado, prominently displayed. I stepped up to the general and pointed to it.

"Je suis un policier," I explained, pointing to my name and then to my own chest. It's amazing what effect symbols of authority have in third world countries. His eyes got very big. He took the wallet and stepped up to show it to his 'Boss Leader' who was arguing with Fred.

Meanwhile, Fred, who sensed the impasse shifting slightly, gave the diplomat a chance to save face. He reached inside the plane, pulled out a couple of packages and proceeded to rip them open.

"See," he explained dramatically, waving the contents in front of the official, "Radio repair parts for this airplane. No contraband." Reluctantly, the official nodded and Fred reached for the release form. Mr. 'Important' initialed it as I was recovering my wallet and shaking hands with the general.

As we climbed aboard and pulled up the door, Fred said, "Let's get the hell out of here before he changes his mind."

With a tremendous feeling of relief we roared down the runway and lifted off for the next stop, Luanda, Angola. Almost due south we flew at 12,000 feet across the Gulf of Guinea where most of our Caribbean hurricanes spawn. Fortunately, the weather was clear and we wondered, as we passed high above Sao Tomé, a tiny tropical island isolated in the gulf, who lived there? Did they wonder about us? Who was it that passed overhead? Where were they from? What were they like? I resolved to check a geographical reference to learn about those folks. I finally did, years later.

Luanda, a metropolitan city of more than a million French speaking people, loomed on the horizon. When we landed we closed our flight plan, ostensibly the end of our long trip. We hangered the plane, went into town for a good meal, a Hilton hotel and a tour of the city. It appeared as if we were there to stay awhile.

Early the next morning we slipped out, caught a taxi to the FBO and bribed a lineman to roll out the Navajo for a 'test' flight. Since the tanks are immediately filled upon landing to curtail condensation with its potential deadly problems, we had lots of fuel aboard. We took off, climbed out and picked up a heading of 120 degrees. At fifteen hundred feet altitude we zipped over a ridge and hugged the surface for an hour or so to avoid radar. By that time we were far enough out in the bush no one cared where we were, nor would they have looked for us if we had gone down. It was not a comforting thought as we brushed treetops, occasionally startling an elephant or giraffe into flight.

With storm clouds building ahead over the Okavonga swamp, we began to climb. At 14,000 feet Fred donned his oxygen mask. At 16,000 he suggested I do the same since we were non-pressurized. I figured it was a good time for me to test my high altitude capability in the event I decided to someday climb Kilamanjaro or Annapurna. At 20,000 I was breathing deeply and easily with no discomfort. 21,000, and then 22,000 wrapped up on the altimeter as we dodged thunderheads. I was yawning a lot but still clear headed, so far as I could judge. (An emergency situation might have proved otherwise). I was satisfied that I could handle that condition, as long as I wasn't exerting myself, so I finally pulled on the oxygen mask. It didn't seem to make that much difference. If I ever get the Himalayan urge, I will remember the feeling of oxygen deprivation high over Africa.

The high, dry veldt had given way to the wet, soggy swamp as the Zambezi River gathered its forces for the plunge over Victoria Falls.

Have you ever been to Niagara Falls? Have you stood on the Canadian lookout point at the lip of the cataract and immersed yourself in the thunder of hydro energy as tons of water plunge to the rocks below? If you have, you'll remember the awesome power and inevitability of the movement. Victoria Falls is five times wider, twice as high and carries ten times more water flow. The local name for the falls derives from its auditory impact: 'Mosi-oa-tumya', the Kololo people's name for 'smoke that thunders'. Even at 2000 feet over the gorge the thunder was audible above the roar of the plane's engines. I have never felt more in awe of Nature's power. We circled the great rift in the earth's surface, caused by a long ago shift in tectonic plates. The spray reached halfway to our wings. We would next see the Zambezi hundreds of miles downstream bisecting the lower veldt on her way to the Indian Ocean. She would be muddy, placid and filled with hippos and crocodiles.

Reluctantly we turned to a southerly heading toward our final destination, Pretoria. The barren reaches of the Kalahari stretched endlessly below us. One of the harshest environments on earth, we carefully monitored the purring turbos, fearful lest we might have to land in that inferno. It was January. That means winter at home. But, the seasons reverse in the southern hemisphere. It was probably 130 degrees down there. No thanks, I'll take a rain check.

The sun was setting over the desert as we turned on the downwind leg of our approach to Wunderboom airport at Pretoria. We touched down smoothly, taxied to the large Piper hanger where we were met by Peter Von der Vooda, the Piper distributor. We handed over the keys and completed the delivery.

After more than 10,000 miles and 50+ hours flight time in four days, we were ready for some R and R. A couple of days later we headed for the bush across the Drakensburg Range into the lower veldt.

But, that's another story.

Trail Ridge Experience

Everyone has a treasured memory of some special place on the planet where a unique, unforgettable experience occurred. It may be an exciting, nerve-tingling instant flash that would never happen again the same way in a million years; or it may be the culmination of a long-planned and well developed program which exceeded all expectation.

Perhaps the most significant and profound ones are those we drift into, not seeming too exceptional at the time; but in retrospect, become watershed events from which all time is measured. Such was the Trail Ridge Experience:

Early in our relationship Jeni had flown to Denver for a long weekend with me. I picked her up at Stapleton Airport and we headed for Estes Park, snug against the front range of the Rockies in the shadow of the towering Continental Divide. Estes is quaint but oriented to the tourist trade, much like Nevada City, California or Cherokee, North Carolina.

We wanted to experience more of the nature side of the mountains, so we left the motel early, breakfasted at a local "watering hole" and headed up into Rocky Mountain National Park. A sizable herd of elk were grazing in the first meadow. We watched them awhile before climbing through different climatic zones to the tundra on top. Trail Ridge road stretched out to the West, the highest through auto road in the U.S.. A lot of it was over 12,000 feet in elevation.

We parked and took a trail leading off around the hill. The wind was blowing fiercely and the wind chill factor was in the teens. We were not dressed for it. A huge boulder appeared which seemed to offer shelter. We settled down behind it with our backs against the rock in the high altitude sun and were instantly warmed.

Two thousand feet below, in a small meadow, a bull elk bugled; big horn sheep grazed just around the cirque; an eagle soared across the azure sky. It was heaven on earth. The pines far below at timberline whispered a melody; a pika industriously gathered grass for the coming winter. All was idyllic for a "time-ignored" period. Then a shout, "Look at them big horns," broke the spell as a tourist came around the rock shouting, but the image remains — indelible.

Often, when we are sitting in a naturally beautiful spot, admiring Nature's handiwork, we compare what we are seeing with our 'mountain top experience' on Trail Ridge. They mostly fall short. So, we enjoy the moment and dream.

Dad, I Wasn't Talking to You

In our early years together Jeni and I lived in a two bed-room mobile home. Marc and Scott were seven and four. They slept in bunks in the middle bedroom.

Jeni often was out of town in her job as representative for a hosiery manufacturer. I became house spouse during those times. The boys and I didn't like for her to be gone any more than she enjoyed being away from the family. But, we managed because we needed both incomes.

One night, after her call from Dothan, Alabama (or some such place), I was putting the boys to bed. Marc slept in the top bunk (less chance of him falling out because he was older). Scott slept all over the lower bunk, end to end, corner to corner, covered and uncovered.

I had listened while Marc said his prayers, which always included, "Keep Mom safe." Then I knelt down by Scott to hear his prayer. He was humming and half singing, rambling all over the verbal ball field. I soon became impatient.

"Scott," I scolded, after he sang to God about the dog next door, the goldfish in the aquarium, the plants outside his window, and all the neighbors by name, "That doesn't sound like a proper prayer to me."

He opened his brown eyes, looked straight into mine and said very firmly, "Dad, I wasn't talking to you."

"Out of the mouths of babes...." How often we get caught up in our scenario of societal conditioning and find ourselves judging actions from the reservoir of our personal experience. What a wonderful thing it is to receive a reprimand from such a gentle and obviously pure intentional source.

It's a lesson I'll never forget. "Judge not...."

You know how you sometimes think you recognize someone, but, upon checking, you discover you've never been at the same place and time as this person? Why do you think that is? Some people credit it to 'look-alikes'. Others suggest previous life connections, or similar types, or mannerisms....

I like to think that what we recognize in another person which seems to suggest we know them, is the Christ Light, the Holy Spirit, if you will, which is Universal. It shines brighter from certain people making them appear to us as previous acquaintances.

After all, are we not all One?

Pigeon Poop

Some days you feel like saying, "Why me, Lord?"

Jeni must have felt that way one bright Sunday morning as she headed out the door for First Christian Church, half a block away. I was already there officiating at the first service. Jeni was singing in the choir and was scheduled to solo that morning at second service.

She was hurrying in order to be on time or a little early to warm up her vocal chords. Just as she reached the sidewalk and turned toward the church a pigeon, perched on a power line overhead, dropped a massive diarrheic load. It was as if he had used a Norden bomb sight. The string of goo plummeted by Jeni's face and hit the cleft of her low cut blouse dead center. It slid right on through to the sidewalk, messing every piece of clothing in its path.

It stunk!

There was nothing to do but rush back and clean up. In record time she stripped to the skin, scrubbed her body pink, doused herself with cologne and redressed. Luckily, her hairdo and facial makeup were spared.

She raced to the church, slipped into the choir loft through a side door and into her seat during the "eyes down" morning prayer. No one was the wiser. But, Jeni, clean as she was, continued to smell the pigeon poop psychologically for a long time.

She's careful these days where she walks.

"This is a Test...Only a Test"

A trusted friend called long distance with a just-received prediction from a 'known-to-be-accurate' psychic that most of Florida was due to sink! He urged us to get-the-hell-out NOW! We lived in Ft. Lauderdale.

We, who had just read Edgar Cayce, were impressed.

A couple of quick calls got us job leaves for a few days. Calls to the boys' schools requesting family emergency leave absences were approved. Then came the decision of what to take and what to leave. It might be permanent. It was a lesson in detachment.

Our source said the psychic predicated her forecast on three earthshaking events which would happen just prior to THE BIG ONE! The first, an earthquake in Japan had happened the week before; the second, a volcano erupted in South America two days earlier; the third 'trigger' was a commercial airline crash in New York which had not yet occurred. It was imminent.

"Time to withdraw ASAP," she said.

Since the friend's call and our leave arrangements had taken the better part of an hour, we didn't want to delay departure.

We decided to take three changes of durable clothes, a sweater and jacket apiece, sleeping bags, towels, paper products, toiletries and what non-perishable food we had on hand. Then came the tools. A small shovel, hammer, pliers, a small hand ax, machete, wire, clothesline rope and nails.

There was a little room left. What other things were irreplaceable? We took the photograph album, a Bible, a few books, 'The Prophet' being one, and some writing materials. That was it. We locked the door on everything else and drove away within an hour.

On the long drive north to relatives we discussed with Marc and Scott the full scenario. We might not be coming back. Florida might not be there. They, of course, were concerned with what would happen to our friends left behind. We had to tell them that some might not survive. Everyone was playing out their own 'game' and ours happened to be just what we were doing. They accepted that explanation.

Well, the plane didn't crash in New York. We had three wonderful days visiting with family in Indiana and headed home. Our guidance seemed to feel the crisis had passed...for now. We also got the very distinct message, "This is a test ...... only a test."

Did we pass? I don't know. I guess time will tell... or maybe it won't.

The Ultimate Perk

There are perks and there are PERKS! I think our best ever job perk came in the mid-70's while I was working as a supervisor for a security guard agency in south Florida. I also sold security contracts to condominium associations and businesses. The company must have been happy with my performance because, after several months of activity, my boss called me into his office.

"Rick," he said, "How would you like an all expenses paid week at L'Esterelle resort in the Laurentians, north of Montreal? You could take your wife but you'll have to pay her air fare."

I said, "Great, but what's the bottom line? What do I have to do to qualify for this windfall?"

"Well," he replied, "You are our best salesman and we have someone up there we want you to visit with. Invite him and his wife to dinner and just do public relations work for the company. You don't even have to sign him up. Just tell him how reliable and responsible our company is."

I knew there was a connection between the Security Company and the resort so I figured the air fare would be their only expense, and maybe not even that, if they used someone's frequent flier miles. But why should I care? With Jeni's $250 air fare and another hundred or so for a rental car we could have a $2,000 vacation.

Off we went - Air Canada to Montreal and a 45 minute drive north to a fabulous dream resort. We were treated as guests of the owner, and, as such, we were not allowed to spend any money. There was a huge fruit basket on the table in our suite with fresh flowers every day and meals a la wonderful.

The P.R. meeting was set for dinner the second night. I explained to the maitre d' the importance of the meal and he immediately took charge.

"Thees night I weel prepare zee finest of seafood eekstravaganzas for you and your guests," he intoned.

At seven p.m. we met our people in the lobby and escorted them to the dining room where we were met by Antoine, the maitre d'.

"Bon jour, mademoiselle et monsieur. Tonight I 'ave for you zee table overlooking zee lake in a quiet corner so you can talk without disturbance."

Our table was ideal, spacious, yet cozy and conducive to quiet conversation.

The wine steward approached and when I asked him to suggest a wine for us, his eyes gleamed as he responded,

"Oui, oui, monsieur. I weel choose for you somesing very special."

A few minutes later he appeared with a dusty bottle cradled in his hands. He displayed it for my approval. I read 'Dom Perignon - 1967' on the label and I solemnly nodded my head. With great ceremony, almost reverence, he opened the bottle. First he handed me the cork for inspection. Then he poured a taster amount in the stemmed crystal goblet. I sniffed it, twirled it and touched it to my lips as if I knew what I was doing before nodding wisely to him to serve it.

Need I comment on the wine? The guests were visibly impressed.

Then came the meal. WOW! Ignore the French onion soup that hinted of herbs known only to God; forget the tossed salad that was as fresh as tomorrow's sunrise; the entree was the 'center stage production'. Let me try to describe it: It was a seafood platter for four, fully a yard long. At each end and in the middle on each side stood two pound lobsters, their tails curled toward the center mound of pink shrimp. Along the edges of the platter, between the large lobsters, were smaller, rock lobsters. The remaining space was filled with various clams, crab legs, oysters, crayfish and other seafood delicacies. The garnishment of leaves, flowers and herbs added just the right visual touch to the olfactory titillation. It was a gustatory Rembrandt.

Words fail to describe the savory tastes, smells, textures and auditory comments of that 'once-in-a-lifetime' meal. I felt like a Roman Emperor feasting on the finest of Mother Earth's offerings.

Needless to say, our public relations effort to establish very friendly connections between our company and the guests was exceedingly successful. They were very pleased with our 'pull-out-all-the-stops' recognition of their importance to our company. Later, back home, my boss was congratulatory on the job we did - but he winced at the bill he received from the resort.

Our primary job accomplished, we spent the rest of the week exploring the Laurentian Mountain ski areas and back roads. We ate in quaint lunch rooms in St. Jovite, St. Adele and Labelle, walked around specialty shops in St. Donat and Laurentides and soaked up the sights and sounds of French Canada.

As we reluctantly returned to Montreal the last day to catch our plane to Florida, we stopped for a delightful visit with 'The Grand Lady'...but, that's another story....

The Grand Lady

For years we had heard our friend, Margaret, speak of 'The Grand Lady'. It was intriguing and aroused more than a little curiosity about the term and the person. The person was Margaret's mother.

How many of you call your mothers, 'The Grand Lady', on a regular basis? Margaret did. So, one day we asked her why. She said she would rather we visit her mother and decide for ourselves.

We finally got the opportunity following our 'Cinderella' vacation to the L'Estrelle Resort north of Montreal. She lived in a small apartment near downtown Montreal and graciously invited us to tea. We accepted with great expectations.

The lady answering our knock was diminutive in size but regal in demeanor. She stood like a queen, walked like a queen and spoke like royalty. She served tea in dainty china with equally dainty pastries. It was a charming experience made more charming by interesting and witty anecdotes from her long marriage.

She agreed she wasn't much of a housekeeper, but that early in her marriage she reached an understanding with her husband that the things outside the house were his responsibility and things inside were her responsibility. This came about one day when John came home and, being tall, noticed an accumulation of dust on top of the buffet.

"Why, I could write my name in the dust up here," he complained.

The Grand Lady drew herself up to her full height, looked him right in the eye and responded,

"Isn't education wonderful?"

They never had another misunderstanding.

The pleasantness of the visit confirmed the title of our hostess. Reluctantly, we bid 'good-bye' to the Grand Lady.

A difficult task can be either an ordeal or an adventure.

Adventurers are winners!

The $400 Dog

Our son, Scott, never accepted the impossible. From his earliest maneuverings he has been a possibility thinker. He would go under, over, around or through any obstacle in his path to reach his goal. This persistence was never more evident than the incident of the $400 dog.

Scott was six and in the first grade at Croissant Elementary School. He walked to and from school along 17th Street and Southeast Third Avenue where we lived. One December day he came bursting into the house, eyes aglow with his newest discovery.

"Mom," he cried, "Can I have a dog? There's a 'PUPPY FOR SALE' sign on my way home and I stopped to look at it. It's so cute and she only wants $400 for it."

We always tried to avoid a direct "No" response with the boys, even when we knew the ultimate answer must be negative. So, Jeni explained that we lived on a busy street, that we had no fenced yard, that we lived in the parsonage and the church didn't approve of pets in the house; but, the best excuses seemed lame to an exuberant young boy. Finally, he seemed to accept the inevitable.

The next evening he came bouncing home with a tiny puppy cupped in his hands. He marched into the kitchen, held out his hands to Jeni and announced,

"Here, Mom, I bought your Christmas present."

How do you refuse a Christmas present, especially from a six year old?

"But, Scott," Jeni protested, "I thought the lady wanted $400 for the puppy."

"She did," Scott replied, "But when I told her I wanted to give it to my Mom for Christmas and I only had a quarter, she sold it to me."

Possibility thinking - you bet!

So, Abigail, sweet adorable dog she became, was with us for a long time and brought much happiness - although none so great as that first announcement,

"Here, Mom, I bought your Christmas present."

Puppy Love

Scott was five and in love. Kim, a neighbor, was also five. They decided to get married. I have no idea what prompted the decision. Maybe that's just as well. Nevertheless, they showed up in Jeni's kitchen one morning with the announcement of their betrothal.

Jeni, hiding a smile behind a "serious" demeanor, asked them where they planned to live. Scott replied, "Part of the time we will live here and part of the time we will live at Kim's house."

When she asked them about money they both assured her they got allowances so money would be no problem. Jeni pursued the conversation asking them if they had considered children.

Scott said, "We've thought about that. If Kim lays any eggs right away before we grow up, we'll step on them."

So, in order to try to discourage the young dreamers without being negative, Jeni suggested they needed to talk to the minister about their plans. It happened we were going down to the church that afternoon for some reason and Scott was with us. (Kim had to take a nap.)

As we walked into the church office, Reverend Kelly was in the office. We were speaking to the secretary when Scott approached the minister and said, "Mr. Kelly, can I talk to you about getting married?"

Bob raised his eyes to ours questioningly. We both smiled and raised our eyebrows. He saw how serious Scott appeared and, since he had no immediate appointments, invited Scott into his study.

Sometime later the door flew open and Scott marched out with an unhappy announcement, "I want to go home."

It wasn't until much later that Bob could tell us the story. Scott had been very businesslike as he pulled a chair up to the desk and sat down. "Mr. Kelly, Kim and I want to get married and Mom said I had to talk to you."

This was a situation the minister had not faced before, a five-year old with wedding plans. So, drawing on his extensive counseling techniques he tried to derail the plan. Scott was adamant and countered every suggestion with a logical answer. That is, until Bob asked him if he had gotten his blood test so they could get the license.

Scott's eyes got big as saucers as he quavered, "What's a blood test?"

Skilled minister that he was, Rev. Kelly spotted a fissure in Scott's well-developed plans. So he mercilessly described the process of drawing blood with a large needle which the nurse would jab into his arm and....

Scott didn't wait to hear more. He lunged to his feet, turned to leave and announced (with tears coming to his brown eyes), "I'm not gettin' married."

Problem solved. We never had to tell him he couldn't. The decision was all his.

To this day he's still single. We'll never know if that encounter was the turning point in his life.

Synchronicity

What's your synchronicity quotient? I don't know if there's a scale or instrument to measure it - but, we've had some experiences that defy the law of chance. Take the Christmas we decided to concentrate our disposable allowance on gifts for the boys, promising not to buy gifts for each other. It was one of our 'less-than-affluent' periods when groceries seemed more important than gifts.

Our 'gift to each other' was to be the trip out to Kansas to celebrate the holidays with John, Louise and their 'grand family.' We felt privileged to be included in their special family celebration.

There was the usual high level of excitement as the expanded family gathered around the tree for the gift distribution. Each gift unwrapped brought a squeal of delight from the kids or 'oohs and ahhs' and 'thank yous' from the adults. We were happy observers to this scene fully realizing there were no gifts for us because we had made a pact not to exchange.

So, we were astonished and bewildered when Dad, who was distributing gifts as Santa's helper at the tree, remarked,

"There's a package here marked 'to Rick,' with no other name on it. And, what do you know, here's another the same size marked 'to Jeni.' It doesn't say whom it's from either."

We each accepted identical gifts, shaped like books and wrapped in identical paper. A glance at each other confirmed the suspicion that we had both violated the 'no gift' pact. As we tore at the paper, the eerie feeling came over us that here was a 'happening.' Sure enough, with no inkling of prior knowledge, we had each gifted the other with identical, hard-backed, blank books. It was time to begin writing. How synchronous was that? We had each longed for such a book without ever sharing the desire with the other.

Pure coincidence — right? Right!

My Eight Word Philosophy:

Hurt Not - Judge Not
Love Unconditionally - Live Joyously

Scott and Father

Scott was a possibility thinker. An eternal optimist, he saw only completed dreams. Any challenge was a project on its way to completion. Such was the case when we lived on N.E. 7th Avenue in Ft. Lauderdale, behind the High School. The North Fork of New River was a block away and an irresistible magnet for Scott's curiosity.

One Saturday he found a boat. Never mind it was half buried in the mud. Obviously abandoned, its aluminum skin was split from gunwale to keel.

"It can be fixed," Scott rationalized.

The first task was to dig it out. I have no idea how long it took. He didn't always share his "newest project" with us until it was well along. The first we knew, Scott was trundling a 14 foot boat down the street balanced on a splay wheeled lawn mower. With no wagon, no cart, no skateboard, no dolly, he used the only thing we had with wheels. Good-bye lawn mower!

My first reaction was, "It's split wide open."

To which Scott countered, "I can fix it."

"But, Scott," I argued, "it's aluminum and aluminum is difficult to weld. Not all welders can weld aluminum. It has to be arc welded."

"Is that what Noah did?" he innocently questioned.

I smiled and explained that we would have to get a trailer, put a trailer hitch on the car, load the boat and haul it several miles to an arc welder. Then he would probably charge us twenty or thirty bucks. Did he have that kind of money?

"Let's go into business together, Dad. We could call it 'Father and Son Boat Business'" begged Scott.

"No," I said, "If we decide to do it, we'll call it 'Scott and Father.' It's your business."

He agreed and we shook on it. As we were discussing it, a pickup stopped in the street. The driver hollered at me,

"Do you want to sell that boat?"

I pointed to Scott and said, "Ask him. He owns it."

He looked askance at the 10-year old Scott and asked, "How much do you want for it?"

"What'll you give me?" Scott countered.

"Ten bucks," was the offer.

"I'll take fifteen," Scott bargained.

The man pulled out three fives. 'Scott and Father' went out of business.

Floating Out to Sea

Jeni had never been to Key West. My enthusiastic description bubbled with 'quaint shops', salt air, fishing boats, Bahamian flavor and flaming sunsets - not just run-of-the-mill gorgeous sunsets, but breathtakingly beautiful events. The far tip of Key West is host every evening to dozens, sometimes hundreds of 'sunset hunters'. My passion was to expose Jeni to this miracle of natural beauty.

So, early in our togetherness, we purloined a couple of days from busy schedules to make the trip down from Ft. Lauderdale. I don't remember where the boys stayed, because we went alone.

The long drive through the necklace of islands was a joy and a pleasure. Jeni effervesced like an excitable teenager in her boundless enthusiasm. Each new island held its own special wonder. An intimate corner of a cafe on the water promised the ultimate in seafood for lunch. Promise fulfilled!

Finally, we ran out of road at Key West and cruised the narrow streets. It seemed to us a cross between Bourbon Street, New Orleans, and Bay Street, Nassau. Few tourists were on the street. Perhaps because there were no tour ships in port, it being a weekday.

We chose a motel which stretched out into the Gulf on a jetty with a sand beach a few steps from the door.

"Let's get into our suits and go swimming," Jeni exclaimed.

We rapidly changed and eased gently into the long shallow surf, slowly allowing the warm Gulf Stream to creep up and up onto our bodies. Finally, about 200 yards out, it was waist deep, so Jeni kicked up her heels to float. She floats easily; I have a heavier specific gravity and tend to sink feet first. (If you saw my size 13's, you'd know why.)

But, I was enjoying just moseying along the bottom beside her as we chatted. Then the conversation faded out and I noticed she had dozed off, still afloat. I continued to walk along beside her, soon noticing the water getting deeper and deeper. I realized *Jeni was floating out to sea!* So, when the water reached my chin, perhaps 20 minutes later, I decided to reverse the direction, not having any desire to go to Havana just then, and gently placed my hand under the small of her back.

The touch awakened her and she started to stand up, but her feet wouldn't touch bottom. She was astonished that she had been cradled in the arms of the Gulf Stream so gently she had slept her way into the Gulf of Mexico. Had I not been there to stop her, she might have floated off into oblivion, never to be heard from again.

Maybe it was the trade winds carrying her away — but, I wasn't ready to trade. So, I rescued her.

"My Hero!"

Grass Clippings

Marc and Matt were buddies. As teenage boys were wont to do, they hung out together most of the time. Sometimes they were at Matt's house - other times they were at ours. It depended on what captivated their interest at the moment.

One summer day they were working on Marc's motorcycle in the garage when lunch time arrived. They came inside to see if Mom would fix lunch for them. She agreed, so they went into the living room to watch television while they waited.

A few minutes later Jeni whipped out a couple of chairside tables and served them chicken salad sandwiches stacked high with lettuce and alfalfa sprouts. Apparently Matt had never eaten sprouts because, when Jeni went back to the kitchen, he whispered to Marc,

"Marc, what's the green stuff?"

Marc, in his usual quick-witted response, answered in the same whispered voice, "Grass clippings. Eat 'em. Mom says they're good for you."

For a long time Matt didn't know the difference — but he was healthier.

Fiat Folly

Oh, how Jeni loved that Fiat convertible! Never mind that it was hard to start, unreliable mechanically, difficult to troubleshoot and a real headache to keep running. When it did run, Jeni was ecstatic. That angel-white beauty, sleek and svelte with its top down, hugged the road like a magnet. Jeni, in her scarlet sweater and scarf, looked for all the world like a maraschino cherry atop a scoop of coconut sherbet. She turned heads.

But, we really didn't need that car. It was definitely an expendable item in our life. So, we decided to sell it. However, Jeni's attachment to the little jewel was not the problem. She reconciled her addiction to it following a trouble plagued trip to Tampa from Ft. Lauderdale. She finally coaxed it home and agreed with me it had to go. Son Scott, our ten year old entrepreneur, had different plans.

We parked it in the driveway with a "FOR SALE" sign prominently displayed. It looked gorgeous with the top down - well worth the $1,000 asking price. Scott volunteered to "detail" it so it would look sharp and irresistible to a potential purchaser. We gratefully accepted his offer, not realizing what he really had in mind. He wanted to keep it in the "family" so, when he was old enough, he could drive it.

We had to go to a Saturday meeting of some kind. I've forgotten what it was. We were gone about three hours. When we returned Scott had totally disassembled the car! The engine was out on the grass, the seats were on the sidewalk, the dash panel was disconnected, control cables and wiring harness dangling free at every opening. It was a wreck.

"But, Dad"' Scott argued, "I just wanted to make it perfect so it would sell easier."

"Can you put it back together?" I questioned.

"Sure I can," he confidently stated.

But he couldn't. All weekend he struggled. The car never ran again. Eventually, I convinced my local mechanic to take it off my hands for a hundred bucks. He said he would tinker with it in his spare time. Scott was in the dog house a long time over that caper.

But, we grow 'too soon old and too late smart,' as the saying goes. Scott grew into the role of master mechanic as a lifetime vocation. Perhaps it was stimulated, in part, by the "Fiat Folly." If so, it was cheap education.

"47"

More than twenty years ago Jeni and I enrolled in a seminar on 'relationships' at Unity Church of Ft. Lauderdale, Florida. The presenter, whom we shall call, Sandy, pointed out that most friction between persons stemmed from *unrealistic expectations*. Her premise was: you have no right to 'expect' your mate to respond in a way *you* deem 'appropriate.'

"For instance," she said, "You sometimes become unhappy and get your nose 'pushed out of joint' if your 'significant other' fails to tell you 47 times a day he or she loves you." She continued her lecture stressing the 'unrealistic expectation' factor time and again.

The following morning, Jeni and I awoke at the same time looking into each other's eyes. Simultaneously we said, '47.' We figured that was a good number of 'I love you's' to start with.

For all the years since, *every day* for us begins with '47.' Some days the numbers reach into the hundreds — and our marriage has become more and more wonderful, perhaps because of releasing 'unrealistic expectations' and remembering to say, 'I love you,' often. For that bit of wisdom we say, "Thanks, Sandy."

Your Presence Is of Great Value

How many of us have wondered, as we proceed along the path of enlightenment, "Where do I fit in? What is my part in the 'Grand Plan'? Shouldn't I be doing more now that I know more? Am I falling short of my 'spiritual duty'?" I know we have.

For a long time we had planned to embark on our "spiritual journey" and "go on the road" with our new enlightenment to fulfill our commitment to the brotherhood of mankind. The trouble was, we didn't have a clear picture of what that looked like in concrete terms. Where would we go? What would we do? How would we spread the "good word?"

One noon, as Jeni was meditating quietly in an unused dental chair of the dental office where she worked, she was agonizing over these questions. Her thought-cry went out to the Universe, "But what can I teach? What will I do to serve? How will I know what to say or do?

I have no degrees; I've not written a book nor taught classes; I have nothing to offer."

The wisdom from the higher planes came rolling and reverberating through the ethers - echoing in her mind:

"YOUR *PRESENCE* IS OF GREAT VALUE!"

The impact of that simple yet profound statement was awesome. It was her answer; and, yet, it was an answer for everyone. She had intercepted it and recognized its TRUTH. But she realized it was both her answer and her lesson to teach.

The important thing is not how much you *know*, nor what wondrous things you *do*, or *say*, or *have experienced*. It is your BEINGNESS that is all important. Only *you* can shine *your* light; only *you* can sing *your* song; only *you* can offer *your* special touch.

"YOUR PRESENCE IS OF GREAT VALUE."

Your handshake or hug can be your blessing.

Life's Right Angle Turn -
The "Spirit of Friendship" Conference

In the late-70's we began to discuss the urge to 'go on the road.' We had no idea what that looked like, but we were talking, dreaming and asking questions. We visualized a time in the early to mid-80's when this could happen. Marc would be away to college or out on his own; Scott would be 'doing his thing', but probably not go to college. It looked like '83 or 84 might be about right. Ah, how plans change when energy is applied.

Here's what happened: Revs. David and Shirley DeForrest from Naples, Florida, came to visit us in their Winnebago. They had begun their 'road odyssey' when they were married some months before. They inspired us! On their way through Ft. Lauderdale, they introduced us to Edyne Decker, whose husband, Nelson, had just transitioned. She had a mini-motor home for sale - but, we weren't ready. We both had good jobs, kids at home and excellent security.

David and Shirley were enthusiastic about a worldwide 'Spirit of Friendship' conference to be held near New Market, Virginia in May, 1979. On the spur of the moment, I decided to attend — Jeni couldn't get off work.

It was *inspiring and motivating*. Such world renowned persons as Buckminster Fuller, Elisabeth Kübler-Ross, Peter Caddy, Swami Kriyananda, Paoli Soleri, Sir George Trevelyan and Paul Solomon presented burst after burst of New Age rhetoric which triggered sky rocket dreams. Man, was I ready! Look out, world — here we come!

I'm sure I broke many speed laws returning to Florida. And, as I bubbled and effervesced to Jeni about this wonderful experience, I said,

"I know we hadn't planned to 'go on the road' for several years, but couldn't we accelerate the projected date from '83-84 to maybe 1980 or '81?"

Jeni never has had a problem making decisions. She's an Aries. Her reply was, "How about now?"

Wow! What a challenge!

My modus operandi is to take it slow and easy. Think about it. Plan all the details. Procrastinate! And, here Jeni was saying, "Let's go."

Think about it. Here we were settled in a home we had recently purchased, a house full of furniture, the accumulation of years of 'stuff' and we were going to pare down to a motor home?

Here's how we did it in rapid stages:

It was May of 1979. 'People just don't buy houses in the Spring,' they said. 'Why not wait until Fall,' we heard. 'You can't just abandon Ft. Lauderdale,' was the cry.

But, we put a 'FOR SALE' sign in the front yard anyway. Nobody called. A week went by, still no calls. Maybe 'they' were right. It's the wrong time to sell it, much less sell it at a price we thought ridiculous.

We didn't know how much we should ask for it. We thought we might add some on to the price we paid for it because we had made some additions. So, for guidance from Spirit, Jeni sat in meditation and asked to contact El Heli, a spirit guide who wrote the book, "The Way to God - Reincarnation," through Rev. Jan Leeboldt.

Almost immediately he was there and Jeni asked what price we should quote. El Heli stated a figure much higher than we would have dared ask. Jeni's first thought was, "That's a lot of money."

87

El Heli responded in her mind, "You'll need it for your trip. It's worth it. Go for it."

Rev. Gina Price, a good friend and noted psychic dropped by for a visit. We discussed our plans with her.

"You'll know you have your buyer when you look out your dining room window and see a rather large lady coming up the walk," Gina related, and went on to describe additional character-istics of the person.

A week went by. A Philippine doctor came by and looked. He seemed very interested. Others stopped by. Then, one afternoon, Jeni glanced out the window and there was 'Gina's described image' coming up the walk. Her first words were,

"Oh, I hope you haven't sold the house."

We hedged our response by saying a Philippine doctor was considering buying it and wanted to bring his wife back. The lady came in and begged us not to sell it until she could call her husband at work to have him stop by in an hour. We agreed and, while we were waiting, took her to the sea grape arbor in the back yard for some iced tea and 'munchies.' Her hubby arrived on time and, after a perfunctory walk-through of the house, came out to the cool, shady yard to visit.

We talked little about the house. Mostly it was just a 'get acquainted' visit. Finally they asked us to delay signing a contract for 24 hours. We agreed and said we were going to be in Margate for a Universal Brotherhood meeting the next night. We could stop by their home in Pompano Beach about 10 p.m. if that wasn't too late.

They assured us it wasn't.

When we arrived, they invited us in and nervously offered to fix coffee or tea. We sat calm and serene, waiting for them to open the conversation. We were supremely confident, having gotten information from other realms through El Heli and Gina that they were our buyers. They, on the other hand, were nervous and ill at ease.

It is said, in salesmanship, when the moment of decision comes, the one who speaks first, loses. It's either a buyer's game or a seller's game.

She spoke first.

"We would like to buy your house," she said. "We would like to offer you....." and she quoted a price $5,000 below our asking price.

We smiled and I responded, "No. We feel the asking price is fair and we don't want to take less."

They looked at each other and said, "We'll take it at your price. It's worth it, but we thought you were supposed to offer less and dicker."

Well, it turned out to be a win-win deal. They were ecstatic with their purchase. And, when the FHA inspector required a new roof on the garage, the buyer helped me tear off the old one and build the new one. We countered by giving them furniture, our master bedroom set and a desk.

When we closed, a month later, the mortgage officer said he had never experienced such a smooth closing. There was no controversy at all. In fact, we took the new buyers to dinner to celebrate.

The House-Car called 'Namaste'

One of the first things we did after making the decision to embark on our odyssey was to go back to Edyne Decker and try to buy her motor home. She invited us for lunch and then we looked the rig over.

The Deckers had used it for their 'on-the-road-ministry' for several years before Nelson passed over. When Edyne heard our plans, she immediately said, "I have been asking $12,000 for the motor home. But, I would much rather you two continue the spiritual work Nelson and I were doing, so I'm going to sell it to you for $8,000."

So, never having driven it, we bought our home for the next five years. Not having any previous experience, I was afraid to drive it home, a matter of ten miles. Edyne's friend brought it up from Hollywood, Florida, the next weekend and parked it in our driveway. For the next three weeks we 'moved in'. I installed hooks, modified closets and arranged storage. 'Gramps' Thomas built some beautiful book shelves. We utilized every nook and cranny. But, I still hadn't driven it a foot.

Finally, we asked UB ministers Winslow and Dorothy Schlosser to help us get 'checked out.' They had a beach home an hour's drive north at Jenson Beach. Winslow drove and explained the various systems.

Push finally came to shove after a wonderful weekend when Winslow said, "Rick, you have to do it sometime or you'll never get out of town. It's simple," he said for the umpteenth time, "It drives just like a car."

So, apprehensively, I climbed behind the wheel and slowly backed into the street. And, you know what? It *did* drive just like a car. By the time we got back to Ft. Lauderdale, I felt like a pro.

The next weeks were preparation weeks, film for the windows, cruise control installation, trailer hitch (we had decided to pull our Honda Accord behind for a 'runabout' car) and a dozen other things. There was so much 'stuff' we felt we needed to have with us. I don't know why. We had been told that our 'Presence' was our ministry — our reason for 'going on the road.'

So, we stuffed the 'stuff', including a top carrier for the Honda, and we were ready to launch. The day following the house closing we headed up the road. In some ways it felt like our ancestors must have felt as they headed west in a covered wagon.

Pioneers again.

The Lesson of Giving

We are told in the scriptures and sacred writings of the ages that we manifest our destiny, that abundance is ours for the claiming, that all good things are ours by divine right, aren't we?

How many of us really believe that? We read it, we preach it, we expound on it - but, when the chips are down, we opt for less. We feel we aren't 'worthy' to have it all. We 'don't deserve' it.

This lesson was brought home to us most forcefully when we were preparing to dispose of most of our 'worldly goods' and take off in a motor home. The house was under contract and we needed to empty it. We thought first of having a garage sale. That would be fun and profitable. But, then, we thought, if we really believe in abundance, why not give it away?

We invited about forty friends to a 'pot luck' farewell dinner on Sunday. As each guest entered, he or she was given labels with their name on them. At dinner we explained we couldn't take much of what was in the house and we had no plans to ever settle down again.

So, after dessert, they were instructed to go through the house and put their labels on the items they would like to have. Then, take them home.

We noticed that one person gazed lovingly at an oil painting and said, " I've always loved that painting,... but, I'll take this vase."

We said, "No, take the painting."

Another said, "I've always admired that tea cart ever since I've known you,... But I'll just take this picture."

Again, we said, "No, take the tea cart."

The scene was repeated time and again. People were willing to settle for less than they really wanted. They felt they should pay us something or 'hold it for us' until we returned. It was *so difficult* for them to *accept* the abundance of life.

What a great lesson — for us in releasing our attachment, but more important, for everyone to test their belief in promised abundance.

Whatever we desire is ours by divine right. We have but to *ask*.

"My Folks Ran Away From Home"

If there was any down side in our decision to 'go on the road,' it was Marc and Scott. We had reluctantly released Scott when he chose to leave home at age fourteen. We struggled with the decision not to force him to stay in private school or stay home. He would just 'disappear' for days at a time. We hoped to maintain a line of communication if we just backed off and let him go. We were 'spirit guided' to allow this.

As Jeni agonized over Scott's behavior while washing dishes one day, her soul cried out, "But he's only fourteen years old."

Immediately a voice from the ethers spoke in her head, "He's no more fourteen than you are. Let him go."

Our 'Presence' evidently was not required for him - or for Marc.

Marc was living at home and working in a motorcycle shop. We told him we would provide a home base for him as long as he stayed in school. But, if he opted to work instead, he could be on his own. We bought him a suitcase for his eighteenth birthday, April 12th, and suggested he look for an apartment.

He thought we were just kidding.

So, when I came back from the Spirit of Friendship Conference and Jeni said, 'Let's do it now,' we were in a position to go for it. Marc didn't believe we would put the house, *his home*, on the market. He was *sure* it wouldn't sell. He thought the financing would fall through. He *refused* to consider a change — status quo seem ideal for him. Free rent, free meals, free medical, and a lot of TLC.

A week before closing we went with him one Sunday and helped him rent an apartment. We had told him he could have any of the furniture because we weren't taking it.

"You mean," he said, "I can have the television?"

"Sure," we responded.

"How about Dad's chair?" as he gazed enviously at my recliner.

"Of course. And, take your bedroom furniture, too."

But, it wasn't until the day of closing that he and Matt, his buddy, rented a U-Haul truck and came for the furniture. As we were driving away, they were driving in to load up.

Forever afterward, Marc would tell his friends, "I'm the only kid I know whose *parents* ran away from home."

Presence

'Presence' is not something you think about doing, or being, or acting out. It is simply your sincere, self-radiating energy. Our first 'taste' of this awareness came a few days after we 'went on the road.'

Mom Vera's friends, the Koehrsens, had a health challenge in West Virginia. We left Deland, Florida, Mom's home, in our motor home heading north toward Wheeling to see if we could be of assistance.

We arrived about five p.m. and were told by neighbors that Virginia had been hospitalized and wasn't expected to survive. We drove there and parked 'Namaste,' the motor home, in a remote spot in the public lot where we could see Virginia's room. Cecil was on terminal watch. We held him and prayed with him. He needed us, he said. Could we stay?

We pointed out the window to where we were parked so he could see us anytime he looked out.

Virginia passed over about dawn. Cecil was calmed, he said, by our 'Presence' in the parking lot. He looked out time and again and was grateful.

We thought back to the time, weeks before, when Jeni had received the guidance from spirit, 'Your Presence is of great value,' and we were glad.

Namaste Says 'NO'

We've always given our vehicles names. 'Old Betsy,' 'Spirit,' 'Louie,' but we named our motor home, 'Namaste' to reflect the higher spirit energy within. Maybe that was why she refused to run in a couple of unusual situations.

The first occurred in the truck parking lot of Little America, Wyoming. (It's on the map - look it up). We pulled into the huge parking lot about nine p.m. and set up for the night. Jeni cooked supper and we turned in. It was November and bitter cold on the high plains just west of the Continental Divide. But, we were cozy with our on-board propane furnace.

The next morning after breakfast we packed up and prepared to roll. I scraped the frost off the windows and noted the outside thermometer read twelve degrees.

Namaste wouldn't start. I ground and ground the starter. Not the first spark. I pulled the bonnet off, which allowed the wind to whistle through the interior. Jeni bundled up and I froze up. I tried everything I knew, including spraying 'quick start' into the carburetor throat. No luck.

We decided to take 'Louie,' the Honda we trailed, and drive back 35 miles to Rock Springs to find a mechanic. No one was interested in making a 'house call' to Little America. The response was, 'We'll tow it in and see what we can do.' That sounded like lots of dollars.

So, we went to the auto parts store and asked for suggestions. The guy sold us a coil and points. (I didn't know Namaste had electronic ignition and had no use for points.)

Our philosophy is, when in trouble, relax and eat some ice cream. We did, then headed back to Little America.

I decided to try one more time to start Namaste before tampering with her 'inerds', about which I knew little. Since I had run the battery down trying to start her earlier, I hooked the jumper cables to Louie and climbed behind the wheel of the motor home. Viola! She started the first time over - no hesitation. We quickly hooked Louie on behind and, since we had gassed up the night before, we pulled out on the Interstate headed for Salt Lake City.

As we entered the top of Echo Canyon we saw spots of black ice - mostly melted. We realized with a shudder that if Namaste had started right up early, we would have topped the rise and slid into the canyon with no traction at all. No power on earth could have held us on the road.

Did Namaste keep us from disaster? Heaven only knows.

The second such occurrence happened later as we cruised around the Monterey Bay area enjoying the warmer weather and anticipating a glorious sunset.

After looking at thousands of Monarch butterflies wintering in Pacific Grove (the only place Monarchs winter outside Mexico) we drove to the sea wall point on Ocean View Boulevard to watch the sun go down. Big signs said, 'NO OVERNIGHT PARKING.' So, we knew we must find somewhere else to spend the night. That was before Namaste intervened.

Jeni fixed a wonderful supper and we dined to the sound of the waves breaking on the rocks and the sun reflecting off the Pacific. After we cleaned up the dishes, we sat on the sea wall watched the sunset and talked until dark, then prepared to leave.

Namaste wouldn't start.

This time we didn't get so perturbed. After several tries, we resigned ourselves to the inevitable. We were stuck in that paradise until morning.

We drove the Honda into town to the police station and explained the situation. We couldn't get a mechanic until morning, we explained, so we asked permission to stay put without getting a citation. They were understanding and left notes for the midnight shift to leave us alone.

The net result was a wonderful night — sea breezes through the open windows, the sighing of the surf with its luminescence, the moon leaving a golden trail to the horizon, and sweet dreams.

Did we need a mechanic next morning? You guessed it — Namaste started on the first turn. We patted her on the dash and said,

"Thanks, Namaste. We believe."

David's Moose

David had never seen a moose. Neither had Shirley. That was one of the main reasons they had come to visit us in the Tetons in June, 1981. They came for three days and stayed three weeks. Then came the momentous day.

It was a beautiful sunshiny day with the mid morning sun reflecting off the 13,770 foot Grand Teton. Breakfast over and my work schedule not calling until 4 p.m., David and I decided to go for a walk. Our motor home was parked in the camp at Beaver Creek, two miles inside the south entrance to Grand Teton National Park. Their motor home was parked in the adjacent space. We told Jeni and Shirley we would hike down the Beaver Creek draw to where it joined the Snake River and follow it to the Moose headquarters. They agreed to pick us up there in an hour and a half.

David was a professional wildlife photographer, having sold some of his prints to National Geographic, National Wildlife magazine and others. He had the knack of catching animals on film at their best. When I asked him how he did it he revealed that he mentally "talked" to each animal while photographing it. He respected the animal's space and time.

We headed down the draw, which soon became clogged with willows and deer browse brush. I suggested he stay up on the high side while I pushed along the bottom in hopes of spooking something out for him to "shoot." I started around a clump of willows and came face to face with a bull moose. He stared at me from thirty feet and I stared back. Remembering

David's technique, I mentally said, "I didn't mean to bother you, old boy. I'll just get on my way," and slowly backed away. I whistled a prearranged signal to David that I had spotted something so he would be ready. When I came out of the draw, there David stood calmly framing and "shooting" the magnificent animal. The bull had come out around the other side of the willows. He actually seemed to be posing as David "talked" to him. Then out of the brush behind him came a cow moose and her calf. The bull grunted at her and she seemed to take up the "game." She nudged her calf who began nursing.

At this point I raced up to the motor homes, a couple of hundred yards away, to get the girls so they could see this unusual event. Number one; bulls never stay with cows and calves. Their "family" contribution is over the previous Autumn during the rutting season. Number two; cows never nurse their offspring in public. And, number three; they just don't stay around very long when humans are present. Nevertheless, we watched David interact with them like a movie director until he finished the 36 frames in his camera. At which time he "thanked" them (mentally) and assured them he would not bother them any longer as he backed away.

If I had not seen it with my own eyes I would not have believed it, but I swear that bull snorted at the cow, she then moved into the willows with her calf and he turned, looked back at David, wagged his antlers from side to side and melted into the shrubbery. It was awesome.

The next day David and Shirley left. They had seen their moose!

'You Can't Rollerskate In a Buffalo Herd'

Don't you wonder sometimes where composers come up with the lyrics to their songs? Years ago Roger Miller sang several unusual songs of his own composition in his inimitable style. One with the lyrics least likely to be realistic repeated the phrase, 'You can't rollerskate in a buffalo herd, but you can be happy if you've a mind to.' Silly, isn't it?

One night I left Signal Mountain Lodge in Grand Teton National Park about two a.m. after closing and putting the night's receipts in the safe. We were living fifteen miles south on Beaver Creek in our motor home. I enjoyed the wee hours drive occasionally spotting a hunting coyote or elk grazing. This night I came over a rise and my lights reflected dozens of eyes ahead a foot or so above the surface. I was mystified as to what they were. No shape or size revealed their identity.

It wasn't until I was within 50 feet that I made out the shape of a huge bison bull as he lumbered to his feet. The herd had bedded down on the sun warmed blacktop for the night and showed no inclination to move. Their shaggy bodies had absorbed all the headlights.

That's when the words to Roger Miller's song sprang to mind. Maybe you 'can't rollerskate in a buffalo herd', but I was about to drive my Honda through. I honked and shouted and finally cleared a path — but, I'll forever remember Roger Miller's words when I relive that night.

Ranger Rick

The summer of 1981 we spent in Grand Teton National Park as night managers at Signal Mountain Lodge, an oasis on pristine Jackson Lake. Jeni was responsible for the operation of the dining room and coffee shop while I had more general responsibilities overseeing the total operation including two gift shops, the grocery store, marina, service station and lounge. We had 55 or 60 young people and some mature couples responsible to us.

Our shift was from five p.m. to one a.m. - or whenever we got everything closed out, the registers balanced and the cash bags lugged across the parking lot a couple of hundred yards to the safe in the office.

One night Jeni was home and I was closing out the operation by myself. Everyone had gone except my two dishwashers whose last responsibility was to sweep and mop the kitchen. I was checking the money bags from different departments in preparation for the trip to the office safe.

Suddenly, a frantic honking outside the front door sent me racing to check the obvious emergency. I envisioned a heart attack victim and rapidly reviewed my CPR training. I hoped the radio dispatcher at Park headquarters hadn't signed off for the night. It was about one o'clock.

When I pushed open the door, the window of the honking car rolled down about three inches and a lady called out, "You've got a bear at your back door!"

My first thought was the two 'swampers' still in the kitchen and I raced back even faster. As I came to the kitchen isle that terminated in the back door, I saw that Mike had propped it open to sweep out and was, in fact, backing up, sweeping his way toward a large black bear. The bear stood with his two front paws inside the door, his head swinging from side to side seemingly deciding which goodies to try first.

I don't remember making the conscious decision to race down the aisle, brush the sweeper aside and startle the bear into retreat. I knew I didn't want him inside the kitchen. Fortunately, he blinked first and backed off ten or twelve feet. I kicked a 30 gallon garbage can at him. It was the only ammunition I had and it worked. He took off at a lope around the back corner which was a level lower than the kitchen.

My next thought was, "Oh, my gosh! My kids are back there."

Several of the young waiters and waitresses were sitting out back talking and drinking beer after work. So, I raced after the bear to keep him moving.

To my dying day I'll remember the startled faces on those kids as we raced by. Some were shouting, "There goes a bear! There goes a bear!" But, another was saying, "Here comes Ranger Rick! Here comes Ranger Rick!"

The nickname stuck. For the rest of the years we were in the Park I was known as 'Ranger Rick.'

Huckleberry Hooch

Did you ever hear of "huckleberry hooch"? I'm not surprised. We invented it. Here's how it happened:

One weekend we drove from our summer home in the Grand Tetons to Twin Falls, Idaho, to visit some friends we met at Signal Mountain Lodge in Grand Teton National Park. We were employed there as the evening managers, which included running the up-scale dining room. People would come for miles to enjoy a superb meal in a fantastic setting overlooking Jackson Lake and the Teton Range.

After dinner they served us some delicious, home made apricot brandy. We tasted it and exclaimed how wonderful it tasted and how smooth it was.

They explained how simple it was to make: put an eight-ounce package of dried apricots into a liter bottle, add a cup of sugar and fill with vodka. It wasn't necessary the vodka be premium.

Every day for three weeks turn it top-to-bottom to mix the ingredients. After 21 days, chill and serve. Yum!

We tried it with such success that we began experimenting with other fruit — peaches, bing cherries and pears. None were as good as the apricot stuff.

Then the huckleberries ripened on Signal Mountain. If you haven't eaten bush-ripened huckleberries you've missed a treat. They are smaller than blueberries, but similar, and grow on low bushes. It makes them easy to pick unless you have to compete with bears, who also love them.

We collected a bunch (without a bruin encounter), put a cupful into a liter bottle with 3/4 cup of sugar and filled it with vodka. After three weeks of inverting we chilled it and — WOW! — ambrosia. We christened the concoction "Huckleberry Hooch."

All Around the Subject:

An aside remark may be an affront if you're taken aback or if it tops yours, and that's the bottom line.

"Hi, Moose"

I wanted to fish the Snake River below the dam in Grand Teton National Park. Jeni wanted to go along, but not to fish. She just enjoyed being out in nature. Never satisfied just to sit, she decided to walk around the willows and sage brush bordering the river picking up cans and paper tourists had discarded. Even in the pristine Tetons careless visitors drop trash. It's frustrating trying to maintain a clutter-free landscape.

Taking her plastic trash bag, Jeni circled up through the brush. As she rounded a ten foot clump of willows, she came face to face with a huge, fully antlered bull moose. A young bull stood close by. The bull stared at Jeni; Jeni stared back. The distance couldn't have been more than twenty feet.

What to do? Many thoughts raced through her mind. Run? Shout? Wave her arms to scare him away?

Not Jeni. She raised one hand, wiggled her fingers and said, "Hi, Moose."

Mr. Moose just stared as Jeni backed slowly away. She was content to sit close by the rest of the afternoon while I fished.

Soccerball Mushrooms

One bright morning in the Grand Tetons I grabbed my ultralite rod and headed for a spot where I'd seen big trout. I hadn't gone a hundred yards until I spotted what I thought was a soccer ball in the sage brush ahead. When I reached it I saw it was a puffball mushroom. I didn't know that at the time, but a call to a Naturalist at Park headquarters clarified it. She said they were edible if that's what we, for sure, had.

The next day Jeni took it to work and confirmed its edibility.

So, I sliced it like a giant tomato, dipped it in batter and fried it like eggplant. Each slice was dinner plate size. It tasted like fried mushrooms. I don't know what I expected, but a soccerball size fungus should have had something going for it besides size. We never found another as large, although we looked often.

It spurred me to thinking. I could raise such mushrooms for the market — a little fertilizer, a dark, cool place and puffball spores. Jeni didn't think much of the idea, so I decided I could go it alone. My business would be called,

'SPORE RICHARD'S ALL MAN ACT.'

Mary of Mount St. Helen's

Being in the right place at the right time was never more true in our lives that an experience in Salkum, Washington. Never was it more important to just BE.

1980 was the year of the BIG BLOW. Mt. St. Helens blew her top and sent umpteen thousand tons of pulverized earth rocketing skyward where it caused all sorts of havoc. Disaster relief flowed from all over the country to those made homeless by the eruption.

My cousin, Janet, and her husband, Jim lived 30 miles northwest and were intimately involved. Jim headed the Sheriff's Department civilian search and rescue team. They manned helicopters, jeeps, horses, mules and light aircraft in search of survivors. Janet organized and managed a food kitchen in the local fire station to feed volunteers, the press and survivors. The outpouring of food and clothing from all over the country was so massive they shuttled vast amounts to other agencies. NBC's 20/20 carried a live segment at the height of her operation when more than 300 people a day were being fed.

We wanted to help, too. But, by the time our summer jobs in Grand Teton National Park were finished, it was September before we could get there. Most of the emergency work had been cleaned up and we settled for a long-delayed visit with Janet and Jim.

Janet took a phone call shortly after we arrived at Jim's real estate office. 'Mary,' we'll call her, a dear friend of Janet's, wanted to come by and talk to her. Did we mind the intrusion?

"Of course not," we reassured her. When did extra people, coming at an inopportune time ever bother us?

At their home for dinner, Mary meshed right in with stories, jokes and conversation. It was so much fun that Janet suggested Mary sleep over, have breakfast with us , then go on to work with Jim. They worked in adjacent offices. We invited her to come back after work and go to dinner with us. We had insisted on taking our cousins to a special restaurant they recommended in Chehalis, about 45 minutes away. She agreed.

The evening was a continuation of light hearted bantering, fun, singing, laughter and fellowship. After dinner, Mary went home.

We drove away the next morning on our odyssey. A week later we picked up our forwarded mail in San Francisco. There was a letter from Mary. She poured out a story to us that was humbling. She thanked us tearfully for our 'presence' in Jim and Janet's home and for our 'presence' in her life. When she had called to ask Janet if she could come by and talk, she had planned to say 'good-bye.' She had decided to commit suicide. Her life wasn't working. A relationship had just ended. She could see no joy in life ahead.

She told us that being with us those few hours had given her courage to live. She saw in us a married couple obviously in love who seemed joyously happy. Maybe it could happen for her.

We soberly looked at each other, tears running down our cheeks, and gave thanks again that our 'Presence' had been of great value.

Yumtatoes

Have you ever eaten a freshly dug, shake-the-dirt-loose, Idaho potato? The difference between such a potato and a store bought, cold storage spud is the difference between daylight and dark, symphony and cacophony. It adds a new dimension to the word 'delicious.'

One September, after our summer jobs as Park Rangers ended in Grand Teton, we headed south and west in our motor home. The parents of one of our co-rangers had a potato farm near Twin Falls, Idaho. She suggested we stop and see them and get some 'real' potatoes.

We arrived about noon and, after coffee and a visit, were asked, "How would you like to follow the potato pickup machine and glean the leavings?"

"Sure," we enthusiastically responded, "We'd like to do that."

So we went to the field where the potatoes were first plowed out of the ground, then picked up, shaken gently to loosen most of the dirt and loaded by conveyor belt into a big truck. The trucks hauled them in to the cooperative storage sheds for sizing, grading and marketing. We watched awhile, then took baskets and followed. In a few minutes we had gleaned a couple of pecks of small to medium potatoes.

Since it was lunch time, Jeni promptly baked a couple of the larger ones in the oven in our motor home. Before leaving Jackson we had picked up some farm fresh butter from a local farmer.

When those golden brown jewels settled onto the plates and we sniffed the aroma we could hardly wait. I think we attacked them more voraciously than good manners might permit — but, no matter, we scarfed them down.

Talk about elixir for the gods — never have I tasted such delicious taters. They shouldn't even be called potatoes they were so good. After devouring the first two, Jeni baked more and we gorged ourselves.

Don't let anyone ever say, 'all potatoes are alike.' Fresh dug Idaho ones are the greatest!

Yumtatoes, for sure!

Tootie Fruitee

We learned a lot those summers we spent in the Tetons. For instance, we learned to convert unsaleable, overripe fruit into wonderfully nutritious dried goodies that lasted us well into the winter. We stopped at a roadside fruit stand west of Jackson soon after we arrived. As was our usual modus operandi we made friends with the owner, Mr. Bender, a Mormon truck gardener from Utah. He asked us if we had any use for a lug of overripe peaches. Wow! Did we! We 'lugged' them home and proceeded to cut, pare, pit, trim and peel our treasure. For days we gorged on ripe fruit — peach cobbler, peaches on cereal, peach nectar and peach snacks.

Then it was 'going-to-town' day again. We shopped only once a week because it was 28 miles to Jackson. We hoped Mr. Bender had something other than peaches this week. He did. He had half a lug of loose white seedless grapes.

He said, "Nobody buys loose grapes. Everyone wants bunches of grapes. Just give me 50 cents for this half a box and we'll call it even."

Well, you can eat grapes — but you can't make grape cobbler, grape nectar, nor eat grapes on your cereal. Fortunately about this time, Donna, who worked with Jeni at Park Headquarters, mentioned she had a food drier she wanted to sell — brand new — for seventy-five dollars.

"Will it dry grapes?" Jeni asked.

Donna didn't know but we decided to give it a try. We washed those grapes, spread them out on trays and turned the drier on to 105 degrees. Two days later we had the most delicious raisins we had ever eaten.

As the summer progressed we collected and dried a wide variety of fruits and vegetables from Mr. Bender. He periodically had pears, apricots, apples, plums, cantaloupes, cherries (its a chore to take out the pits), figs and bananas. The fruit that was too ripe to slice, Jeni put in a blender and pureed. She then poured it on waxed paper covering the trays. It dried to delicious fruit leather. It was so rich, though, that a little was all one could handle at one time. We used it for 'hiking energy'.

By the time our summer tour as Park Rangers was over we had dried a substantial cache of delectables. We gave a lot away as hostess gifts as we traveled the country. But, we were still eating dried fruit through the winter and into spring.

Bing Cherries

There are still wonderful, trusting people in the world you don't have to meet personally to know and appreciate. When you encounter such a person, it adds a sparkling facet to life. We enjoyed just such an exhilarating experience one autumn in a most unexpected place.

After our summer jobs in the Grand Tetons ended in September, we headed northwest through Yellowstone National Park toward Washington. En-route, we intended to visit Glacier National Park, one of our dream spots.

At Missoula, Montana, we parked 'Namaste,' our motor home, in a regular mobile home park. We usually parked in truck stops or roadside rest stops. Early in the morning we headed north in the Honda toward Flathead Lake. Flathead Lake acts as a heat sink for solar radiation. That's important in far north Montana. There's a late Spring and an early Fall in that country. The predominant northwest winds blow across the lake carrying water-stored sun energy to the eastern shore. What a garden spot!

It was a bright and clear Sunday morning that we were enjoying immensely. We began to see roadside fruit and vegetable stands but none of them were manned. Then we realized we were in Mormon country and everyone was in church.

The vegetable plots turned into orchards. 'Pick your own cherries' was on every sign. We couldn't resist the big red orbs beckoning us from every tree. So, we turned into a farmyard. I went up to knock on the door of a small but neat bungalow and found a note pinned there. It said, "We've gone to church. Go to the sorting shed and get a basket, then pick the amount of cherries you want. Weigh them on the scales inside the shed and leave the money on the table. They are twenty cents a pound. The best ones are on the trees at the back of the orchard."

I went into the shed for a basket and noted several piles of money on the counter. We picked and ate — ate and picked, then weighed out about twenty pounds of the ripest, sweetest, best tasting cherries ever. We left our pile of money with the rest (a little more than we needed to) and drove away with a sermon on human nature in our experience. I wonder how many other piles of money were more than they needed to be? Probably most of them.

We tell this story time and time again reinforcing the honesty and goodness of people — if you give them the opportunity.

Strawberry Biscuits

Yum! (Son, Daryl, says it's superfluous to say it twice.) But, we could have said it six times and still not given the situation the accolades it deserved.

We were returning from the Tetons and the ancient Indian Medicine Wheel in Wyoming across the northern states toward Michigan's upper peninsula. Early one morning we drove out of Fargo, North Dakota headed east.

'Pick your own strawberries,' the sign said. It sounded good but we didn't want to take the time. We were headed for the source of the Mississippi River. Nevertheless, we turned in and drove to the packing shed. The lady said, "No, we don't pick and sell retail. However, someone left a basket full in the field last night they must have forgotten. I'll let you have it for a couple of dollars if you have something to put them in."

We quickly emptied a box and filled it with vine-ripe strawberries. Boy, were they good — sweet and mushy-ripe. We ate some, then stopped up the road a couple of miles at a Hardee's restaurant for buttery biscuits. The sweet, grandmotherly type at the drive-up window said, if we could wait five minutes we could have fresh, hot biscuits. Of course we waited.

Never, in all my many years of sampling and gorging the world's delicacies, have I tasted such a wonderful combination as sweet, vine-ripened strawberries on fresh, hot-buttered biscuits.

Add a few yums for nostalgia.

Marc

I want to attempt to tell our son, Marc's, story as best I can. It won't be easy:

Marc was a near legend, not among his peers, for they never believed his exploits, but among the aviation community who were generations older.

Marc first flew with his grandfather Harris in a Cessna 172 when he was 13 months old. 'Pap-pap' strapped him in the right seat and off they flew. Marc promptly went to sleep - what a cradle! In the next few years 'Pap-pap' would periodically come by the house to pick up Marc and they would be gone most of the day, flying from airport to grass strip to airport. Marc came to love flying as an addict loves a 'fix'. He became known as 'Pap-pap's copilot' among the hanger crews.

We moved to Florida and for several years Marc's 'flying career' was on hold. The exception was a Delta 727 flight to Atlanta for a family visit. He and his younger brother, Scott, flew by themselves under the watchful eyes of the Delta steward-esses. Jeni and I were the only ones who suffered trepidation. Marc surely didn't. As soon as the seat belt sign was turned off Marc was on his way to the cockpit. He convinced the stewardess to introduce him to the flight deck crew. Marc was a small-statured eight year old with a lot of confidence as he told them he was his grandad's copilot and that they flew Cessnas all the time. An amused but very interested crew answered his questions about lift-off airspeed, flap controls, compass heading and ground speed. 'Pap-pap' would have been proud of his 'copilot'.

School wasn't Marc's favorite pastime. He begrudged the time spent in the classroom when he might have been out playing with model planes or watching airliners on final approach to Ft. Lauderdale International airport over our house. Any time we would be driving as a family to or from somewhere, he would always beg me to take the 'old short cut' by the airport, which usually was miles out of the way. But, because of my interest in flying, I usually agreed. His one good year of school from kindergarten to high school sophomore, when he dropped out, was the year he spent at Florida Air Academy. That was a great experience for a fourth grader who absolutely knew he was destined for a flying career.

The summer he was ten he 'found' his mentor, Al Heasley. As the summer vacation drifted into its second week, Marc complained he was bored. There was nothing to do.

"Marc," I suggested, "Why don't you ride your bike out to the airport and get a job?"

"Wow, Dad, do you think I can?," he shouted.

"Maybe some Fixed Base Operator needs a 'go-fer' " I said.

"What's a 'go-fer'?" Marc asked suspiciously. He was well aware of my propensity for joking.

So, I explained that some mechanics might like to have a kid like him to run to the stockroom for parts so that he didn't have to interrupt his job. The runner could 'go for' the parts, hence the term, 'go-fer'.

Next morning early he packed a lunch and off he went. Many turn downs and negative responses later he finally connected with a salty old mechanic who had been a Master Sergeant line chief in the Air Force. I guess Fred recognized the enthusiasm he might have had at that age and told him he could hang around. At any rate, Marc became a regular at Red Aviation (although there were probably those who considered him a nuisance). He would take his lunch and pedal off each morning returning before dark tired and greasy, but with sparkling stories of engine changes and preflight checks. Having been an aircraft mechanic in WW II, I could listen with attentive interest and cogent comments.

One evening he rushed in all breathless and excited.

"Dad," he babbled, "I met Al Heasley today. He flies a Cessna 401 for some corporation and he wanted to know if I wanted a ride on a check flight. I said 'sure', but he said I would have to get a waiver from my folks. What's a waiver?"

I explained that it was a release of liability form we would sign so, if anything happened, Al and his company would not be held responsible.

"Can I have one?" he begged.

"Sure," I said, and wrote out a waiver which Jeni and I signed. He was ecstatic!

The next day he took his first flight with Al, a furloughed Pan Am captain, who was flying a corporation Cessna. It was the first of many as Al, recognizing the potential of the young boy, began to school him in the correct safety checks and eternal vigilance of a good pilot. They flew together in small planes and large, Cessnas and Lockheed Electras, Beechcrafts and Lear jets, until they ended their careers together twelve years later in the fiery crash of a Galaxy Airlines Lockheed Electra at Reno.

It was a ground crew error. Someone had left the 'air start' door open as the fully loaded plane's turbo-jet engines were spun to start. The crew was aboard and the plane was buttoned up for takeoff so none of the flight crew was aware of the catastrophic error until the plane reached flight speed. Then, the vibration was so intense from the 'scooped up' air through the open air start door that the plane was only airborne ninety seconds before bellying into a field where it hit propane tanks. They blew up on contact. Of the seventy aboard, one survived. It wasn't Marc.

The 'in between years' for Marc were a series of challenges and adventures. Not all of life was a bed of roses. He dropped out of high school, wrecked the Hondasaki motorcycle he custom built, barely escaping with his life, nearly starved and probably tested the drug scene. But he never strayed long from the flying career.

Al called one day. Marc was fourteen.

"Marc," he said, "I've got a job as a copilot on a Lear jet. Do you want to be my crew chief?"

"Man, Yeah," Marc shouted. "What do I have to do?"

"Mainly you have to be at Executive airport when we have a charter flight and make sure the food and drink bar is stocked for the clients we are flying. Sometimes we will need the 'over water pack' when we are flying out of the country. And, occasionally, if we are just flying a courier run, you might get to go along."

"Wow," an excited Marc yelled, "When do I start?"

So began the Lear 25B chapter in his life.

Harvey Hop was the chief pilot and charter manager for the owner, Harry Mangurian. Harvey had more cockpit time in Lear jets than any other pilot in the world at that time. He chose Al to be his copilot because of his 10,000 hours logged with Pan Am Airways and others. As top-of-the-line professionals, Marc couldn't have had better mentors. Public school began to interfere more and more with his 'real' schooling. He had few contemporary friends because no one his age could relate to his 'flying career'.

When he would arrive at school on a Monday morning with stories of his weekend flight to Houston or Montreal or San Juan, the kids would hoot and holler at his 'bragging' and go shoot baskets or smoke pot. Imagine their skepticism the morning he told them he had dinner in Houston with Neal Armstrong and Buzz Aldren, the astronauts. (Harvey was a longtime friend of the early group of astronauts and frequently interacted with them. Marc was a tag-along.)

For the next couple of years Marc's life was a kaleido-scope of events and experiences few people can even dream about. One such flight was the Bill Cosby charter from Ft. Lauderdale to New York. At that time Cosby was the principle advertising voice for Jello on TV and radio. After takeoff and climb out to 41,000 ft., the uncontrolled altitude above the airliners, Harvey handed the controls over to Al so he could go back and visit with Bill. That was his modus operandi when transporting celebrities. Soon a prearranged plan unfolded. Harvey called Marc, who had quickly replaced him in the cockpit, and suggested he serve refreshments. Marc brought back a napkin covered tray and presented it to Cosby. He whipped off the napkin to reveal a mold of Jello quivering and vibrating on the plate.

"Oh, no," grinned Bill, "Take that stuff away and bring me a sandwich. I'm Jelloed out from all those commercials."

Harvey enjoyed pulling pranks on celebrities. Marc just wasn't impressed by titles or reputation. He would much prefer to sit in the cockpit absorbing his flight education than to 'bask in the glow' of a big public name. An exception was Bill Cosby who, Marc said, was 'real'.

One time they were flying Paul Newman somewhere and, as usual, Harvey was visiting with him in the cabin while Al and Marc flew the plane. Harvey called Marc on the intercom and said, "Come back here, Marc. I've someone I want you to meet."

Marc reluctantly left the controls and went aft.

"Marc, I want you to meet Paul Newman," he announced.

"How do you do, Mr. Newman," Marc politely responded.

Harvey felt that Marc wasn't responding with enough awe and enthusiasm so he explained, "Marc, this is Paul Newman, the famous movie actor."

"I hope you are enjoying your trip, Mr. Newman," Marc replied. "Now, Mr. Hop, can I get back to the cockpit?"

Paul burst out laughing and patted Marc on the shoulder. Here was someone who didn't give a hang about his 'public image'. He loved it.

Marc didn't often volunteer information about who they flew - only about the flight itself, the plane's performance and the stopovers. As I would pick him up after a call from the 'in-flight' phone (often at two or three in the morning) I would pull out of him who they carried. Sometimes it was Jackie Gleason or F. Lee Bailey, sometimes it was the Shah of Iran's family members or some big name politician whom Marc didn't know, or care to.

He might say, "Oh, you know, Dad, that singer. I think his name was John Denver."

Then Al got a new job and again took Marc along. This time it was to crew a Lockheed Electra turboprop for Dr. Rex Humbard, the Christian evangelist. Neither Al nor Marc were particularly religious so the ground rules were established early when the minister attempted to 'lay his theology' on them.

"Mr Humbard," Al said, "You preach and I'll fly. That way we'll all get along fine."

Rex did - and Al did - and all was peaceful.

When the evangelist was not 'on tour', he chartered the aircraft to individuals and groups. Consequently, Marc got a lot of international flights and experiences in foreign lands. He was 18 or 19 at the time and living his life to the fullest.

One day he called us with big news. We were working as seasonal Park Rangers in Grand Teton National Park in Wyoming.

"Dad and Mom," he announced excitedly, "Will you guys come to Florida and marry Chris and me?"

He and Chris had been dating for some time so it wasn't a surprise. We agreed to head south as soon as our season ended in mid-September. Maybe it was prophetic that the ceremony was delayed and almost didn't occur. The rehearsal was a test of patience for Jeni. She wanted it to go smooth and perfect. It was a circus. But, the wedding did go smoothly, except for grease on Marc's tux. Somebody, I've forgotten who, had car trouble. Marc, with his usual concern for his buddies, fixed it. After all, first things first.

The marriage lasted a couple of years, hit some rocky roads and stuttered. He and Chris were trying to patch it up before his last trip. She had moved into the house we had co-rented with Marc just days before.

During this period in the early eighties, Marc progressed rapidly in his profession. He graduated high in his class at flight engineering school at Opa Locka. He was on a roll, superb aircraft mechanic, conscientious flight engineer, careful pilot. His boss at the time, Phil Sheridan, told us after his death that never in all his long aviation career had he ever seen such a natural aviator and mechanic as Marc.

By 1984 he was flying regularly as flight engineer for Galaxy Airlines. Al was the Chief pilot. They were flying charter groups to Las Vegas and Reno as well as junkets to sporting events in that last month.

January 20th, 1985, that last fateful day, they left Las Vegas returning a gambling charter to San Francisco. After the Super Bowl in Candlestick Park they returned a charter group to Seattle then flew empty to Reno. After refueling, they loaded a gambling charter group to deliver to Minneapolis, then return to Ft. Lauderdale home base for a much needed rest. Marc had been gone six weeks.

It wasn't to be.

The people were boarded, doors closed, the crew in place and Al signaled the line chief to start the fans spinning with the compressed air generator. The props wound up as the crew checked the preflight list. All the gauges were in the green and Al signaled to disconnect the umbilical. They were ready to taxi. But, the line person who disconnected the air start tube couldn't reach the access door to fasten it closed.

She later said she intended to ask the crew chief to secure it but another task grabbed her attention and she forgot .

The curtain descended on the lives of 69 that night. Marc moved into a higher career.

It was devastating for Jeni that Marc had preceded her to the next dimension, but she handled it as well as a mother can, under the circumstances. She was in Rio de Janero with Dr. Barbara Vitale attending a world educator's conference when she got the news. Pan Am Airlines provided her a first class ticket because her return ticket was unusable immediately. She arrived home to face a life without her first born.

The aviation community, sparked by Harvey Hop, organized a memorial 'fly-by' on the Ft. Lauderdale beach the following Sunday. Six Lear jets flew along the beach in front of the hotel verandah where the families had gathered. One plane was missing in the formation, as was traditional.

Marc was gone physically, but he was only a thought away. Many incidents occurred which proved to us that he was 'still around'. The day of the accident I got the call from Galaxy Airlines about 6 a.m. that there had been a crash. I dressed and rushed out to the airline offices at Ft. Lauderdale International airport. They broke the news that all the crew and 65 of the 66 passengers were gone. (The 66th passenger, a 17 year old boy, had miraculously survived. His seat was ripped from the floor and he was thrown clear of the plane, which burned. He unstrapped his seat belt and walked to the approaching emergency vehicles.) The Galaxy staff was distraught. I consoled them as best I could before going home to notify Jeni and family.

The press, always looking for a story, zeroed in on the mentor/student relationship held by Al and Marc for twelve years. They questioned me long and in detail about Marc's life-long obsession with flying. The phone rang off the hook with calls from newscasters and reporters.

By 11 p.m. I was exhausted. I put on my pajamas, turned out the light and stretched out on the bed. The telephone message recorder beside the bed suddenly clicked on. The phone hadn't rung, the machine just started, ran about 30 seconds and clicked off. I was puzzled, particularly when I replayed the tape and heard nothing on it. Then I thought, 'Ah ha! That's Marc getting in touch with me'. I replayed the machine several times and decided there was no other explanation. (I've wished since that I had taken it to a sound engineer to see if he could enhance it and pick up anything). But, I just said mentally, 'Thanks, Marc. I got the message'.

The second evening I had finished the chores in the living portion of the house, turned off all the lights and retired. Jeni still had not gotten back from Rio. The next morning I walked into the living room and the table lamp over Marc's picture was turned on. Again, I breathed thanks to Marc for the contact.

Jeni had frequent contact with him from the first evening while still in Rio. He would pop into her mind, say something typically 'Marc' and either stay around to talk or pop out. Many things he said to her the first night were very typical. Jeni was always urging the boys to take their vitamins. They called her, 'My Mom, the Pill Pusher'. Jeni had fixed packets of vitamins for Marc before he left that last time. He said to her, in thought, 'And, Ma, I didn't take my vitamins'. She had to laugh through her tears at the thought.

There are many more stories and anticdotes I could relate, but this has given a reasonable picture of the boy/man Marc was. He was doing just what he wanted to be doing when it came his time to 'buy the farm', as they say in aviation circles. He was only 23, but he had lived a full and exciting life. Others are content to push brooms or punch typewriter keys; Marc experienced the world. We are happy for him and release him to the next level.

The Atlanta Move

"If they play senior softball in Atlanta, I'll move with you," I tongue-in-cheek remarked to Jeni. (If truth be known, I'd probably follow her through fire and brimstone, if she decided to go.) She said she would call someone and check it out.

We had decided to move from South Florida sometime earlier — but Jeni had finally gotten the intuitive message loud and clear — 'GET OUT OF THE WHIRLWIND IF YOU WANT TO CONTINUE TO LIVE.' It had disabled her physically until she arrived at the point of decision whether to stay in this physical plane or leave. She felt she had more to do in this life, so she decided to stay. But, to do so meant she needed to leave 'status quo,' move from our beautiful home near Little River in southwest Ft. Lauderdale, a home we loved, and relocate elsewhere.

During our vagabond years from 1979 to 1984, while roaming the country in our motor home, we looked at many areas as 'future nesting sites.' I think Jeni always had in the back of her mind to settle down again. After our 1984 season in Grand Teton National Park we did.

We spent two years back in Ft. Lauderdale recovering from Marc's death and again 'jump starting' Universal Brotherhood Movement. But, Jeni never let go of the basic motivation that caused us to leave Ft. Lauderdale in 1979 and 'go on the road'. She was never comfortable again in South Florida. All the while we were dealing with Marc's death and subsequent events, Jeni was getting more and more energy depleted.

Finally we chose to go on vacation to Stowe, Vermont, because we could trade our 'time share' week for one there the last week of October, 1985. It was to be a three week trip through Atlanta, where our son, Scott, had just moved, then on to New England.

Jeni announced she was taking her clothes and her car as far as Atlanta because she wasn't returning to Florida. Her decision was clear,

"If I go I can continue to live, if I stay here, I'll die," she said. There was no choice.

A visit with Scott confirmed Atlanta as the place to move. He was a part of the picture, but other factors played a big part, too.

We had listed on our 'new home requirement' sheet such items as:

1. A four season moderate climate.
2. A younger median age group.
3. A dynamic economy.
4. An airline hub.
5. A major population center.
6. And perhaps the most important criteria — lots of trees.

Atlanta was the first of all the cities we 'previewed' while traveling. We looked favorably at San Diego, Tallahassee, Florida, Santa Fe and a couple of other places.

We chose Atlanta. Jeni stayed while I returned to Florida to wind down our activities (in lay language that meant, 'finish the softball season').

And when I asked Jeni to check about senior softball, she was shuttled from pillar to post until she finally reached Pam Taylor, Supervisor of Special Populations, Bureau of Recreation, for the City of Atlanta.

The question, "Do they play senior softball in Atlanta?," brought this response from Pam,"No, not yet. But, we just had a staff meeting this morning and decided we needed such a program. Now, I've got to find someone to run it."

"I'm married to the guy who can do it better than anyone," Jeni replied. "Do you want to call him in Ft. Lauderdale?"

When Pam called, I told her I was coming up to spend Thanksgiving with Jeni and asked if we could meet. We arranged to have breakfast at Shoney's Thanksgiving morning. Jeni and I were waiting when she arrived. It seemed perfectly natural for me to step up, introduce myself and hug her. (Doesn't everyone hug the person who is interviewing them for a job?) In Shoney's I specified 'NON SMOKING' to the hostess and didn't know until after our two-hour breakfast conversation that Pam was a heavy smoker.

The net result was, I was hired to start in January, which gave me time to finish the softball season in Ft. Lauderdale, play in a state tournament and move.

"Wow!" I told Jeni, "Last week I couldn't even spell 'recreation specialist' and now I are one." Life is strange.

Hi - De - Ho!

One of the many joys of being a Minister is the joy of officiating at weddings. To sit with the groom and the best man while the bride's preparations move endlessly toward perfection is a study in human nature. If the groom is nervous, the best man usually carries on a running conversation to help ease his tensions. If the groom is calm and cool, more often than not, it is the best man who is up and down, nervous because the groom isn't.

"How come you're not bitin' your nails, man? Don'cha know you're supposed to be scared?," worries the best man.

Then, there's the suave, cosmopolitan man-about-town who wants to be different - and spectacular. Such was the case of one whom we shall call, 'Pete.'

We arranged to meet 'Pete' and his bride on a summer Sunday at daybreak in an open field. Fifteen or twenty guests also showed up for the event. Then, into the open area drove a pickup pulling a trailer containing a huge basket. Out of the pickup came a large, tarp-like bundle which unrolled as a hot air balloon envelope. The groom, best man, minister (me), and some of the guests helped unfold and smooth the panels.

Next came the basket which was set on its side and attached to lines from the envelope. Into the basket came the 'engine,' a device which looked like a construction site propane heater. Some of us held the neck open while the pilot fired up the burner and aimed it at the inside of the envelope. Bye-and-bye enough hot air puffed the bag that it began to lift to a vertical stance. Soon it stood inflated and ready to fly. The wedding could now begin.

There was only room in the basket for the bride, the groom and the pilot. I had to stand outside as the guests gathered around. We were ready to start but the trouble was, nobody could hear over the roar of the engine. So, the pilot eased back the throttle to a delicate balance necessary to maintain lift with minimum noise. I *still* had to shout.

"*Dearly beloved,*" I began.

As the bride dimpled sweetly and the groom hung on to the rail they each lip-read my words and repeated their vows,

"*I, Pete, take thee...*"

I've heard of shouting good news from the housetops — but this was hilariously ridiculous. I shouted,

"*Do you take this woman to be your wife....*"

He yelled, "*I do.*"

I know she echoed him because I read her lips.

At the grand finale, as I pronounced them man and wife, the groom gathered his new bride into his embrace (still holding the rail with one hand) and the pilot opened the throttle.

What couple ever drove away from their wedding 'chapel' in a more glorious limousine? Off, off and away into the sunrise sailed the beautiful carriage, too far to throw rice but just right for blown kisses.

Mismatched Duel

The towering cab of the 18-wheeler loomed ominously over the roof of my diminutive Toyota as I drove north on I-85 into South Carolina. Suddenly the turn signal on his fender blinked and he eased into my lane. With no shoulder to my right I had no place to go. I hit the brakes and horn at the same time his great front wheel crunched into my fender. I realized I was below his rear view mirror and he couldn't see me.

Disaster was imminent.

It had been such a beautiful trip since leaving Winder, Georgia, following a week-long senior camping event I helped stage. The sun was just past its zenith. I was listening to a cassette of Chopin on stereo. The Toyota Supra our son, Scott, had rebuilt was on easy cruise control. It was rocking chair music for sure.

The long upgrade didn't affect my cruise control. But, the 18-wheeler barreling along in the center lane past me seemed to be slowing down. A quick glance in the rear view mirror revealed a white sedan rapidly closing the 300-yard gap behind the truck. There was a third inside lane she could have used for passing. But, who knows what prompts a driver's actions? This trucker decided to clear his lane so the white car could continue on through. At the precise instant he made his decision, the turn signal flashed and he turned the wheel. I was the unseen factor in the equation.

The initial bump startled him but he couldn't identify the source. He had totally forgotten he was passing me earlier before the grade started to slow his speed. His reaction was to hit the brakes and continue changing lanes.

He hit me again!

This time it was solid. The door post bent, the windshield cracked and I spun 90 degrees to the line of travel — right in front of the diesel. That chrome grill, blocking the view a foot from my nose , was unnerving. I slid sideways down the road inches from his radiator until he bumped me again, spun me 360 degrees across three lanes of traffic and into the concrete median wall. There I sat, stunned, not believing I had survived a duel with an 18-wheeler. I flexed my arms and legs; there were no broken bones . No blood dripped anywhere, so I closed my eyes and breathed a prayer of thanks.

By this time the truck had slowed to a stop up the road and the driver was running toward me. The driver of the white car had also stopped opposite me and she came dashing across the highway to see if I was hurt. I smiled at them, crawled across the center module (because my door was jammed against the median) and stepped out, obviously not laughing.

A cell phone 911 call from a passing motorist had already alerted the highway patrol. He appeared on the scene moments later and sized up the situation. Since I didn't need ambulance transportation, he put us in his cruiser to sort out the details. I told my story first. Then the lady from the white car, obviously an angel, explained that it was all the truck driver's fault. How often would an eye witness to an accident stop to corroborate your story of the events? She did, bless her heart.

So, the patrolman, the truck driver and I went back to my car and assessed the damage. We bent the fender away from the wheel so it could turn and checked for further damage. I climbed back in, started the engine and found it could still run. The trooper said there was a tire and body shop at the next exit three miles up the road if I could drive it that far. I did, slowly. The mechanic, shaking his head ominously as I related the story, began to check the engine, the steering, the alignment, the electrical and other systems. Miraculously, nothing was mechanically out of whack enough to prevent my continuing my trip. He adjusted the alignment slightly and pronounced it suitable for the road even though it had a smashed headlight, broken windshield and unusable left door. Can you believe, when I asked how much I owed him, he said,

"You've already been through enough. There's no charge. Drive carefully and stay out of the way of trucks."

Did I turn around and go back home? Of course not. I was on my way to play in a senior softball tournament in Annandale, Virginia. I went on, arrived late at night, but in time to make the opening game the next day.

Oh, how did we come out? We won!

Rhinoceros

Max, our Chinese grandchild (by heart adoption) was four and spoke only his native language. His Chinese grandmother, who had named him 'Little Dragon,' as maternal grandmothers were permitted to do, was satisfied with his monolingual capability. His mother, Elaine, our (heart adopted) daughter, felt he should learn English if they were going to stay in this country. She realized he could not compete without it.

Every day Max came to our home so Jeni could teach him English. He progressed rapidly under her tutelage. He was very bright (aren't all 'grandchildren'?)

One evening I arrived home to the joyous shouts of, "Grandpop, Grandpop! I can say English." He climbed on my lap as I relaxed in my easy chair and I picked up an 'International Wildlife' magazine. I turned the pages and successfully coaxed Max into looking at the pictures and saying 'zebra' and 'bear.' Then I came to a rhinoceros.

I said, "Max, this is a rhinoceros; say rhinoceros."

Max looked at the photo and remained silent.

Again, I said, "Max, say r-h-i-n-o-c-e-r-o-s ."

Again, Max was silent.

"Come on and try," I pleaded.

"Say r-h-i-n-o-c-e-r-o-s."

Max turned on his knees in my lap to face me, placed his tiny hands on each side of my face, looked straight into my eyes and said, very emphatically, "Grandpop, say r-e-f-r-i-g-e-r-a-t-o-r."

Do You Know Jesus?

I had just left the City of Atlanta Bureau of Recreation offices on the sixth floor of the old converted mill on Forsyth Street. The elevator stopped on the fifth floor and a solemn individual joined me dressed in 'sincere blue.' Before the door had fully closed he addressed me in a sepulchral voice,

"Do you know Jesus?" he intoned.

I'll never know what possessed me to say it but I asked, "Does he work for the Bureau of Recreation?"

The startled evangelist stammered,

"Why, he works for everyone."

I responded, "Oh, sure I know *him*. The carpenter. He helped me build some shelves in my garage last Saturday. If you see him, you tell him Rick said 'Hi'."

The elevator door opened. I stepped out leaving a speechless preacher standing there with his mouth open.

Tsk, tsk, should I be ashamed?

Quan Yin Appears

Quan Yin is a legendary lady. Protector, guide, ancient goddess, enigmatic, she's known and revered by many in both Eastern and Western philosophies.

Jeni, whose chosen name in Mandarin Chinese means, 'she who loves people', felt a warm attraction to her. She wanted a Quan Yin statue for her 'Angel Room', a healing sanctuary in our home. We looked several places without success.

Then, sometime later, we were in Colorado for Universal Brotherhood ordinations and visits in Denver, Boulder and Estes Park. We were meeting Shir Lee Duncan from Aspen in Boulder to ordain her at the home of her friends one evening but could find no hotel or motel vacancy. Some Colorado University function had filled all the available rooms.

So, after the ordination, we drove north on State Highway 9 toward Estes Park. At Lyons we spotted a 'vacancy' sign and pulled in. It wasn't fancy, a 'Mom and Pop' type motel with only about a dozen rooms, but, it looked clean. We registered for the only unit left, Number five. (The numerologists among you will recognize the number five as 'travel and adventure.' There are a lot of 'five's' in our lives.)

We parked in front, grabbed our suitcases and unlocked the door. The light switched on and there, across the room at bedside as a table lamp, was a sixteen inch statue of Quan Yin. What are odds of finding a Quan Yin statue in a small, ultra conservative mountain town in Colorado?

Pure coincidence, right? Right!

"Oops, Time Out"

Senior softball, played at tournament level, is just as competitive and intense as major league ball, albeit somewhat short of that quality. Intramural league play, however, is a bit more relaxed and, while competitive, produces a lot more fun and good humor. The game is played to win — but it isn't a 'life-or-death' event as some consider the championships to be.

One evening at Best Friend Park in Norcross, Georgia, our team was playing another league team, the second game of a seven-inning double header. We had lost the first one nine to eight in a see-saw contest that ended with the game-winning run in the bottom of the seventh. We determined to even the score the second game. Tied at six going into the bottom of the seventh, it was our last at bat. Fleet-footed Ray walked and took second on a bobbled infield ball. With two out it was our best chance with a man on second if the next batter could hit the gap in the outfield. He did! Billy slapped a screaming line drive to right center, obviously a hit. Ray left second, sprinted toward third and was waved on by the third base coach. As he thundered toward home plate, Curtis, the right- center fielder, in a heroic effort to cut off the winning run, raced in, grabbed the ball in his throwing hand on the first bounce and, with all his forward momentum behind it, fired a rifle shot to the catcher.

Ray was four strides from the plate when the unexpected throw slammed into the catcher's glove. He skidded to an upright halt five feet short of home base while the rest of the team groaned from the bench. In a totally unexpected act, Ray placed the upright right hand in the palm of the horizontal left hand and shouted, "TIME OUT!" He was so serious and tension on everyone was so great that both teams exploded in laughter, including the catcher holding the ball. He fell to the ground in uncontrolled mirth.

Ray, the only calm player on the field, stepped on the plate untouched.

We won, 7 to 6.

Jeni heard my heart thumping
in Morse code.

Author's Note

I wrote these stories, mostly in longhand, as I sat in my lounger in front of the TV, alternately watching the Atlanta Braves and penning memories. I've often thought of the wonderful life I've had. I was born into an ideal family, grew up in a loving home, was encouraged to stretch my imagination and wings, and released into LIFE. For this I am eternally thankful. My fondest desire would be that everyone could be so fortunate.

Perhaps, as you read these reminiscences, they will stimulate your memory to recall some of the best times in your life. It is my understanding that we are here to be joyful and experience happiness, that the world's best and all its abundance are here for our asking. I've asked for and received the best. Life is good. May it be so for you.

Happy trails

Notes:

From YOUR Joy of Living experiences.
Record your memories & good times here.

Notes:

From YOUR Joy of Living experiences.
Record your memories & good times here.

Notes:

From YOUR Joy of Living experiences.
Record your memories & good times here.

Notes:

From YOUR Joy of Living experiences.
Record your memories & good times here.